Overcoming: Overwhelmed
How to Get Unstuck from Life's Challenges

**Simple Secret Strategies to Get Your Life Back
There is an Overcomer in You!**

By Daren Carstens

CaV
CARWAYNE
PUBLISHING

www.carwayne.com

ISBN 9780989371612

Cover Designer: Adam Carstens

Digital Book(s) (epub) produced by Carwayne Publishing

Why You Need To Read This Book

Do you feel stuck? I am going to help you overcoming being overwhelmed and get you into your flow and into your go! You are going to live a life of significance, purpose passion and fulfillment.

Life has a way of overwhelming us, with to-do's, problems, and circumstances. What I have discovered, is that when we are overwhelmed, we become paralyzed, and then we put off the actions we need to take to reach our dreams and goals.

This book is about how we change those feelings, and emotions that slow us down derail us year after year. I am going to share with you the keys, I have found that separate those who move forward, grow and reach their God given potential.

Do you feel like no matter how hard you try to make changes in your life; something always keeps that from happening?

Are you struggling to lose weight, stay happy, move on, or start a new adventure in your life?

If this is you, then "Overcoming: Overwhelmed" will teach you exactly how to get to a place in your life where you are walking around with a smile on your face from sunrise to sunset.

"Overcoming: Overwhelmed" is a step-by-step guide that will get you from down in the dumps to the top of the mountain, and then you will learn how to stay there.

Filled with inspirational messages, how-to ideas, quotes from great Overcomers and stories that will motivate you to take the next step toward reaching your goals, Overcome: Overwhelmed will help you get to the next level.

Whether you are looking to move up in the business world, save your marriage, pull yourself out of depression, lose weight or quit smoking, "Overcoming: Overwhelmed" will help you find the Overcomer inside of you and stomp those bad habits into the ground.

This book is full of ideas, facts and steps to take that can help you succeed in all the areas in your life.

Gaining the power of an Overcomer is easy and everyone can do it! Whether you want to be on top financially, with your health, or in your business, this book will teach you tricks of the trade that will have you waking each morning with a smile on your face and a heart that is ready to conquer the world. Before you know it, YOU will be an Overcomer that is teaching others how to overcome generational curses, addictions, depression, anger management issues and any other hardship that comes along.

Discover the power of making your dreams come true with "Overcoming: Overwhelmed".

Personal Note from the Author

This book comes out of personal experience in the pursuit to overcome the overwhelming obstacles and circumstances I have faced in my life. Having gone through divorce, and remarriage, blended family situations, financial hardships, and the list could go on and on. I am a pastor that has worked with thousands of people through the years to help them overcome and make it through the overwhelming circumstances and situations that so many times cause defeat or at least hold us back from reaching our potential. I have discovered some simple keys, that if applied will set you free from being overwhelmed and help you reach your potential.

That is why I put together this success guide called "Overcoming: Overwhelmed. My passion is seeing people just like you, overcome the hardships of life. This book will help you unlock the secrets to being an overcomer; there is an awesome overcomer in you. Within the pages of this book, you will learn these simple yet secret strategies to get your life back, and get unstuck from life's challenges.

Daren Carstens

INTRODUCTION

OVERWHELMED
o·ver·whelmed (Verb)

1. Upset, overthrow
2. a: to cover over completely: submerge
   b: to overcome by superior force or number
   c: to overpower in thought or feeling

DO YOU FEEL STUCK?

Does it seem like no matter how hard you try to make changes in your life, something always holds you back? Are you struggling to lose weight, stay happy, move on, or start a new adventure? Life has a way of overwhelming us, with to-do lists, problems, and all kinds of crazy circumstances. I've discovered that when we feel overwhelmed, we can become paralyzed, and we put off the actions we need to take in order to reach our dreams and goals. This book is about how we change those feelings that slow us down and derail us year after year.

In this book, I am going to share with you the keys that separate those who move forward, grow, and reach their God-given potential from those who don't. You'll discover exactly how to get to that place where you're walking around with a smile on your face from sunrise until sunset.

"Overcoming: Overwhelmed" is a step-by-step guide that will take you from being down in the dumps to standing on top of the mountain, and show you how to stay there. Filled with inspirational messages, practical ideas, quotes from great overcomers through history, and stories that will motivate you to take the next step toward reaching your goals, "Overcoming: Overwhelmed" will help you get to the next level in your life.

Want to move up in the business world? Save your marriage? Pull yourself out of depression? Lose weight? Quit smoking? This book will help you find the Overcomer inside of you and stomp those bad habits into the ground. Before you know it, YOU will become an overcomer, teaching others how to destroy generational curses, addictions, depression, anger issues, and other roadblocks that stand in their way to greatness. Discover the power of making your dreams come true!

OVERCOME
o·ver·come (Verb)

1. Succeed in dealing with (a problem or difficulty).
2. Defeat (an opponent); prevail: "they overcame the guards"; "we shall overcome".
Synonyms: overpower - vanquish - conquer - defeat - surmount - beat

"Pray like it all depends on God, but work like it all depends on you." - Dave Ramsey
Welcome to Overcoming: Overwhelmed. As you can see above, an overcomer could mean a lot of things. Being an overcomer could mean that you are a winner. It could depict you as a conqueror, a champion. I do know this that God says this about you: *you are an overcomer*.

God declares you, he identifies you, he views you, and he has a snapshot picture in his mind of you as an overcomer. My goal and my role is simple: I want to get you to see yourself in the way that God sees you; to see yourself as an overcomer. In this book I am going to give you a profile of an overcomer. If we were to go to God's dictionary and look up the word overcomer, my prayer is that you would look at the profile of what an overcomer (the definition of what an overcomer is) and that you would see your picture there. I am going to help you get to a point where you so identify with the character traits and the qualities of an overcomer that you learn to see yourself as that person. That's my prayer for you. I really want to challenge you to look at this profile of what an overcomer, a winner, a champion and a conqueror is, and to see yourself that way. There are some great promises in God's word.

Do you know that all overcomers, all conquerors and winners, have a common denominator? Do you know what the common denominator is? It is a word called adversity. Every conqueror must face trouble and opposition in order to be an overcomer. You have to have opposition. God never once said that this would be easy. I would love to be an overcomer without adversity. Wouldn't it be great to have the glory without the battle, without the fight, and without the discipline? I would love to have the jersey and the trophy. Would it be as fulfilling to win the championship game without having to go through the trials of two-a-days in 100 degree heat? You practice in the morning and then you practice in the afternoon. It's August and school hasn't even started yet, but you're going twice a day. By the end of the week it seems like it's all you have done all day, every day. Then if you have a personality like mine, you played all night in your dreams, leaving you without reprieve, exhausted from the sense that you never had a break. I was lucky enough to have friends that didn't play football and found that taunting me was a much better way to spend their summer days. They would drive up with a big glass of water and they'd point and laugh after taking a big gulp of sustenance. And there we were, sweating, out on the field practicing, trying to defeat dehydration. In order to be who God says that you are, you're going to have to go through trials and tribulations. What I am going to teach you is how to see yourself as a person who conquers, as a person who wins, as a person who is a champion.

The book of Revelation says a lot about an overcomer.
Revelation 2:7 Whoever has ears, let them hear what the Spirit says to the churches. To the one who is victorious, I will give the right to eat from the tree of life, which is in the paradise of God.

The prizes that an overcomer will get from God will surpass any trophy or medal. *You* get to eat from the tree of life; *You* get to escape the second death; *You* get to rule in authority with Him over nations; *You* get to never lose your place in His kingdom. As an overcomer, you will sit on His throne with him and deny the accuser, the one that tells you that you're nothing that you'll never make it. You get to inherit the kingdom and all of the benefits along with all of the promises of his kingdom, they belong to you! You overcomer you! That's what you get that's who you are! It doesn't matter what you've done, where you've been, who you have hurt. God has a place for you in His kingdom and he is waiting for you to overcome.

When Is Pay Day?

All of the fruits of prosper and delight belong to you. This is not a novel or a mystery. This is the real world, full of real adversaries. But the real God says that you're an overcomer, he sees you as an overcomer and I want you to see yourself as an overcomer. It's time to start obtaining and receiving these prizes today. They are yours! There's something important about seeing the prize and knowing that it is coming, that a pay day is coming with God.

God doesn't always pay every Friday, though I wish he did, but the payday is coming, and you will reap a harvest if you stay in the game. You stay in the game! Romans 8:37 is a famous verse that follows another famous verse that we quote all the time at my church. The first famous verse that we quote all the time is Romans 8:28, which says this: *God takes all things that you go through, good, bad and the ugly and he works them together for good for you who love him and are called according to his promise.*

God can take the mistakes of your past, the horrible things, the tragedies and the heartaches, all of the junk of your past, God can take that and turn that into something good.

Then we come to verse 37 where it says this: *amid all of these things, what things? These hard things, amid all of these things, we are more than conquerors and gain a surpassing victory through him.*

Right through him! It doesn't happen on our own, but it happens through him who loves us. My encouragement to you is this: You're a conqueror and you've got the victory, amid all of these troubles, you've got the victory. I want you to see yourself as victorious. Paul teaches us that all of us are in the race of life, and the problem is that a lot of us want to arrive at our grave safely so we tip-toe through life avoiding hardships and uncomfortable situations in hope that we safely arrive at our grave at the end. I want you to know that is not the life that God has for you. There are hurdles that you have to jump. There is a long jump, there is a pole vault, and there is a shot put. This is a race that we are in. We are in this race called life and there is opposition in this life. What makes you a conqueror and what makes you a champion is the fact that you go through them and that you're not a sideline person. Don't just relax on the bleachers of life, instead, be in the game. Some of us are not in the game though.

Sometimes we don't view ourselves as being in the game. I want you help you to see yourself in the game. In 1 Corinthians 9:24, Paul says that we are in a race that everyone runs, but only one person gets first prize so run your race to win! To win the contest you must deny yourself many things that would keep you from doing your best. An athlete disciplines his body and faces strong opponents just to win a blue ribbon or a silver cup, but we do it to win a heavenly reward that never disappears. So I run, Paul says, straight to the goal with purpose in every step. I'm not just shadow boxing or playing around, and like an athlete I punish my body, treating it rough and training it to do what it should do, not what it wants to do. That's why we do things like fast. We ask God for wisdom in our lives, we dedicate our upcoming days to God and fast in order to prove that dedication. A fast doesn't have to mean food. Some people fast television or media. One guy came up to me two years ago and he said *"Pastor, Pastor! I discovered what I'm going to fast. I'm going to fast marijuana this year. I'm not going to smoke pot this year for 21 days!"* I love that I am the pastor of the kind of church where someone feels comfortable enough to come to me and say, *"Hey, I'm going to quit smoking weed for 21 days."*

God did not give us the right to judge. It is his job alone to judge. So I didn't condemn him. I just gave him a little shove towards the finish line by saying, *"You know what? I think you can make it past 21 days. How about trying it for 30 days and then if you make it that far, go for more! Come on, you can do this and I'm with you."* Here's the point: Yes, I'm encouraging you but I am also encouraging myself. Right now my body wants to go eat some doughnuts; lots of them; doughnuts with sprinkles and filling and little flakes of coconut. Yeah I'd love to do that. You know what else I'd love to do? Go eat some doughnuts and then go to bed. And then I want to get back up and eat some more doughnuts and then I want to go watch football. I know that my flesh wants to do a lot of stuff that will keep me from experiencing God's best. It's not just my flesh's appetite, but it is also the things that I want. I want to be lazy, I don't want to work hard, I want to do this or I want to do that. Here's the deal: Paul says we're in a race. Run your Christian race, live this life as a Christian who is competing to win. And by the way, you're not competing against other people. Do you know who your biggest battle is with? It's you!

Stake Out The Competition

You're competing against yourself. I want you to see yourself and I challenge you to see yourself through this book, Overcoming Overwhelmed, as a person who is just that. Sometimes you're going to read something that you're going to say; that ain't me. I don't even identify with that character trait. At that point, I want you to think to yourself that that may be a fact, but the truth trumps the fact. Have you ever played Spades? In the card game Spades, the ace of Spades is the highest, it trumps everything. Boom! I don't care what card you've got, the ace of Spades trumps it. Whatever the facts are in your life, the truth of God's word is the Ace of Spades and it'll trump every card. A guy said to me the other day, "*I'm only happy when I'm high. I only have purpose in life when I'm high.*" I think that he expected me to say "*that's not the truth!*"
I agreed with him and I told him that he was probably right. Somewhere in his life, he had an emptiness, and was filling it with a substitute. They only thing that was filling that hole was the utopia that his mind created when he drank and did drugs. There's pleasure in sin for a little while, that's what the Bible says, otherwise sin wouldn't be tempting to us. The whole deal of it being tempting is even a little bit of pleasure. Filling that hole with sin meets a need for a little while, but the truth is that it's just a substitute. The truth is that God has a plan for your life. The enemy is trying to derail you and distract you because he wants to win just as bad as you do. Truth trumps the fact every time. So what do you do?

What makes a champion is that we've got to have some great desire. First and foremost and number one is that desire. Passion. I know a man that trains Navy Seals. He has told me that for most who attempt to be a Navy Seal, it's the prestige and the title that they want. It's the elite of the elite of the elite of the fighting military men and what an honor it is to be able to say you are a Navy Seal. As a trainer he said this: "*I know if you give me a hundred guys and these guys are physically fit, most of them trained, pre-trained to even get there, out of one hundred guys, only ten of them will be left at the end of my camp. My goal is to find out if there is any quit on the inside of anybody. I'm going to get the quit out of you, if it's in you I'm going to bring it to the top and the guys that don't have any quit, they come out the other side, they're the cream that rises to the top, they're the winners, they're the champions and what I'm looking for is this: I'm looking to find out if you've got any quit. I hope you don't have any quit, but I'm looking for it. Because I can't have you...my job is to train these guys, I can't have them quitting on the battlefield."*

So I'm going to rough you up right now to find out if you've got the quit on the inside of you. What is it that makes someone not quit? Let me tell you, it is passion, it is dream, it is a desire that overcomes obstacles, adversity.

Hebrews 11:1 Faith is the substance of things hoped for, the evidence of things not seen.

You're sitting in a chair and you don't need to have faith for a chair because you already have one. You are in it. What you need faith for, is a dream; you need faith for something that's not in your life right now. I hope you have a dream, I hope you have a goal, I hope you have passion.

Why are YOU on Earth?

Dave Ramsey made a video where he talks about why he thinks God put him on Earth. Dave Ramsey feels like God put him on planet earth for this reason: to get the body of Christ and the church out of debt, away from the bondage of debt, because debt keeps you from sleeping good at night, it steals your joy and keeps you from funding the gospel, the kingdom, doing what God's will is for your life. When you need something and you're in debt, you can't always get it. God wants us out of debt. Dave Ramsey feels like his passion and his purpose in life is to help the body of Christ see the same picture that he sees for them. Dave provides an example when he is speaking to live audiences. He's on stage and a gazelle is running across the screen behind him. The audience can see the gazelle running but what they don't see is the lion chasing the gazelle. What Dave is saying is that you have to get a passion and you have to get a dream. Find your desire and run, run, run! You may not know it but you are being chased! And he's bouncing across the stage and he's cheering and going nuts and some people think that all of that ruckus is unnecessary. I just want you to know that it does take passion, because when opposition sneaks up from behind you and all hell breaks loose, if you don't have passion, you will quit. It is really that simple. You won't stand a chance. If you don't have passion when it gets hard then you may as well hit the bench. And on the bench is where the splinters come from. Get in the game!

How many of you watch college football? This past year for the first time in history, a freshman won the Davey O'Brien quarterback award and the Heisman Trophy. I told my wife about it, she's not really a football fan, but I told her about this kid and I just so happened to turn the TV on and there he was. Johnny, they call him Johnny Football. You look at him he looks like a normal guy. He could be sitting next to you and you wouldn't even notice him. Just an average built guy who doesn't look like that much of an athlete, not at all jacked up and beefy, he just looks like one of us. He fits in with the norm of society, but let me tell you, this kid is so not normal. If you watched him play football, he was a freak. Not because he was an outward freak, but because of what was going on down in his heart. This kid is an animal on the field. He plays with such passion that the Holy Spirit was preaching to me while I was watching this kid play football.

What most people don't know is that he was arrested just a few months ago for wrong conduct. He got in a fight while trying to break up a fight. Does that make him any less of a person? Just because you go through some hard times doesn't mean you're still not a champion on the inside. They interviewed his coach and he said that he had a conversation with Johnny, explaining that he wasn't even the starter, he was just the backup. After all, he's a freshman and a senior was a starter. But by chance that senior got hurt, putting Johnny in the game. He said that during the first game he brought him over and said *"Johnny, this is a football. You better learn how to handle this football or you won't be playing anymore."*

After that talk something amazing happened. What was on the inside of that kid came out. It was an inspirational message to me because I know that many of us go through hard times and many of us get a slow start in our race. A lot of times it doesn't look like we're going to make it, but it's not how you start baby, it's how you finish the game. This race we're in is a marathon, it's not a sprint, and you've got to have great desire.

How do you do it? First and foremost, you've got to connect to the Lord.

Psalms 37: 4 Take delight in the Lord, and he will give you the desires of your heart.

All of the goals and dreams that you have, the things you really want, are possible. Commit your way to the Lord, roll and repose each of your cares and your load, trust in Him, lean on Him, rely on him, and be confident also in Him. He will bring it to pass. Listen, endure, play with heart, have desire, have a dream, have some goals, and have some want, too. Want to see something happen. Are you with me?

Be Healthy

It's time for us to deny ourselves. This is who you are destined to be and I see you this way. God sees you this way; and my prayer is that you see you this way. Number two, you have a healthy mindset, a great attitude. This is a battle for us because this battle is won or lost right there between your two ears. You win or lose by what you allow to go on inside your mind. You need to start by developing a great attitude and a great perspective. You have to be able to admit when you're wrong and get it right. One of the great things a person can be is self-aware. In the Twelve Step Program one of the things that you do is you have to admit that you've got a problem. As long as you mask it, as long as you hide it, it will still haunt you. Admit to yourself: I'm deficient in this area and I'm weak in this area, I'm struggling in this area, I've got an issue, I've got a problem. When you admit it, you can begin the process with hope.

Proverbs 28:13-14 Whoever conceals their sins does not prosper, but the one who confesses and renounces them finds mercy. Blessed is the one who always trembles before God, but whoever hardens their heart falls into trouble.

What is a healthy spirit? It could be said this way, *healthy thinking, a right perspective, a healthy attitude conquers adversity.* The cool thing about God is that he gives us the opportunity to participate in the outcome of our life. In fact, God lays out a plan for you and he makes a path for you, but the outcome really is on you. He has given you free will. Sometimes I don't like that because like I said, I want those donuts in my bed. I want to say to God, *"God you know my address, send the money in the mailbox! Let me sleep!"* I don't want to go to work today, but God says no, I want you to be fruitful and multiply. He also says that we have an outcome, and that we have an input into the outcome.

Matthew 9:29 According to your faith, my faith, it will be done unto me.

Tell yourself, *"I've got to develop my faith and I've got to develop my own attitude, I've got to develop my own thinking, I've got to build my faith muscle so that my outcome is what I want it to be, my dream is what I want it to be and I've got an input into the output."* Number three, I have to have strong plans, goals, dreams, and a game plan. No football team, no baseball team, no hockey player, no wrestler, no MMA fighter goes into the challenge without a plan. Everybody comes to the game with a plan. Every baseball team says okay, you're better at pitching so you're going to pitch. You're fast so I'm going to have you bat in this order of the lineup. You're a good fielder so I'm going to put you at short stop and then you're a home run hitter so I'm going to put you in clean up. What is that? That's called a game plan.
As followers of Christ, I want you to see yourselves as people with a game plan. Be dedicated followers with goals that help you fulfill the game plan that God has for your life. Being a pastor, I ask people all the time, *"What do you want God to do in your life this year, what do you want to happen?"* Eight out of ten times I will hear one of these two words or noises, it's hilarious. The first is, *"Aaaaaa…"* if that was a word. They're pausing because they really

don't know. Or they use this word, "*Well...*" What that answer means is: "*I haven't thought about it.*" As Christians, we ought to be able to roll off our tongue what we want because we all should have some secret desires and some petitions inside. Faith is the substance of things that I'm hoping for and it's not here yet, but I'm hoping for it. I'm certain and I have an expectation that it's going to happen. I've got a churning, a passion on the inside for what I want to see God do.

This year at my home church we're going to start a mentoring program. I'm going to work with some men and I'm going to filter the applicants so that the participants are going to have to be serious but not curious, because a lot of a people are curious and once they know what's up, they're out. Yeah I'm curious about that pastor. Well I'm going to filter out the curious and get to the serious. If anyone in my church has a serious need to be mentored by me, they'll have that chance. I'm going to filter through and eliminate the folks that just want to get to know me. I want people who are

serious about changing their world. Not because the curious are not valuable, because they are, but sooner or later you've got to get serious. And if those patrons are serious, then we're going to do some great things together.

TAKE ACTION

- Tell yourself each morning, "I'm An Overcomer!"

- Look up the profiles of some famous overcomers like David, Bethany Hamilton, or F. Scott Fitzgerald.

- Try to come up with some ideas on what God might want from you as an Overcomer.

TABLE OF CONTENTS

Chapter 1 | The Secret of a Goal

Chapter 2 | Heart Trumps Talent

Chapter 3 | Heart Trumps Talent Even More

Chapter 4 | Happy on Purpose

Chapter 5 | Entitled To Be Happy

Chapter 6 | Write It to Right It

Chapter 7 | Be Inducted Into the Faith Hall of Fame

Chapter 8 | Less Drama, More Momentum

Chapter 9 | Get Down With LTP

Chapter 10 | Hands Free Zone

Chapter 11 | Re-Educate Your Mind

Chapter 12 | Compounding Breakthrough

Chapter 13 | Brokedown Habits

Chapter 14 | Student of the Game

Chapter 1
OVERCOMING:
OVERWHELMED
The Secret of a Goal

The greatest enemy to human souls is the self-righteous spirit which makes men look to themselves for salvation. -Charles Spurgeon

I have set a lot of goals for myself and for my church this year. I'm working toward the development of a first-class children's ministry where your kids are wowed. Do you know that we can reach the parents by reaching the children? They will be dragging mom and dad to the church. And wouldn't it be cool to have full time staff that does nothing but minister to the children? Yes! So, do I have some goals and some dreams? Absolutely!

My dad, when he was facing his battle with cancer before he died, did not have a goal to stay here. There were a lot of people around him who didn't understand that. They thought that he should believe for healing. They wanted him to believe so that he could stay. And he's there saying, *"I don't have anything that really like inspires me that much anymore, I'm ready to go to heaven. I'm like Paul was, I'd rather be there than here."*

If you want to stay here and if you want to be effective and if you want to be an overcomer, a winner, a champion, a conqueror, who I say you are and who God says you are, you've got to have a dream, a passion, a goal. Job said in Job 6:11, *but I don't have strength to endure.* In other words, he did not have strength of battle. Why? There isn't a goal that encourages me to carry on. The battle's too intense; I need to have something on the other side of the battle worth fighting for. My love for my dad had me screaming *"Dad, come on, you can beat this, you know, go through chemotherapy, get your radiation, do some treatments, come on, hang in there. Fight this fight; you can believe God, God is a healer, he heals, we see healing go on all around. I said come on get a dream you can work with me."*

But he simply said, *"I'm done with that, boy!"* I kept coming up with dreams and goals for him, *"Come on you can write books. Come on dad, you can work with leaders."* But those were goals that I wanted him to have, not goals that he had. He was done. He was ready. And because he was ready to go, he went. He's not here. He's better off but we miss him. I wish that he would have fought for something, but he didn't want to. But that's the thing about God. He had given him the choice. You can't make someone do what they don't want to do. In his mind he had fought those battles, he had turned the ministry over already and he said, *"Man, I'm going to watch the rest of this from heaven. I'm going to go to heaven."*

Hebrews 12:1 Therefore, since we are surrounded by such a great cloud of witnesses, let us throw off everything that hinders and the sin that so easily entangles. And let us run with perseverance the race marked out for us.

There's a great cloud of witnesses that are in heaven, cheering us on as we run our race, screaming go, go, go! I think of my dad up there, *"Go, go Daren, go, go, get 'em, come on Enjoy Church, come on!"* And what I'm saying to you is that since we are here and since we are in our race, let's not live in the grandstands before we get to the grandstands. You're not going to have these battles, opposition and adversity in heaven. You've got them now. You need to be an overcomer now, not when you get to heaven. Yeah you'll get the prize then, but now is the time that you're on the mat, you're up to bat; you're running, hitting the hurdles of life. You're an overcomer! You're an overcomer!

Part of overcoming is being able to see the problems. Proverbs 27:12 says that a sensible man, watches for problems ahead and then he prepares to meet them. A simpleton never looks and they suffer the consequences. Paul says, *"I strain towards what's ahead, my eye on the prize, I'm going forward, I'm going to make it, come on, press in, God has called me heavenward."* That's where we're going, right? This is not home for us so let's fight, fight, fight with a great attitude and with strong plans.

Finally, you have to have great bounce back ability. You are the comeback kid! Now, if you really want to convince me of that, you've got to do this. You have to live with a passion that makes others believe that you believe. You stand in front of them saying, *"I know I've been bloody. I know have had the snot beat out of me. I know I've been through some stuff. I've made some mistakes, but I've got comeback on the inside of me. I have a strong bounce back response. I'm not giving up."* When I was a kid one of my favorite toys was the little clown punching bag that had the sand in the bottom. I don't care how hard you hit, in fact, the harder you hit that thing the faster it'd come back up. If you hit it soft it would go down slow, but man it had a great bounce back response. You are that. You're a clown that bounces back. That's who you are.

In Galatians 6:9 Paul says it this way, *"Let's not become weary in doing well for at the proper time we will reap a harvest if we don't give up."* So what I want you to know is that it is payday with God. He does pay, and he pays well. If you sow you will reap, and you cannot out give God. Whatever good you're doing, keep it up, keep on sowing, keep on serving; keep on doing, doing, doing, doing, doing what's right, because you're coming back. You are going to reap your harvest, you're the comeback kid! You've got a great bounce back response, boom! The devil knocks you back, boom! You can't even help yourself, you just come back. I hope you see that about yourself and believe that's who you are.

Next, you need to start talking to yourself. Here's what I know, everybody talks to themselves. Some of us whine, *"Oh! Woe is me!"* and life is rough. You may be in church and you confess, I can do all things through Christ who strengthens me, and then you go out the next day and feel like nothing good ever happens. You may feel that you never get a breakthrough. And what I want you to know is that God sees you as a person who has quality self-talk. He is steadfast and you must be patient.

Biblical Science and Talking To Yourself

Can I get all scientific with you for a minute? I love science. What I love about science is that the Bible always confirms science. Science doesn't confirm the Bible. Scientists tell us this; that the biggest battle you will ever face in your life is not with the devil. It is not with the enemy of your soul, although he is an enemy.

Science says that the worst enemy you'll ever face is your own self, your own ego, your own self-talk. The enemy "in-a-me" is the worst enemy. What is your ego? It is your left brain, the analytical mind that filters everything through logic and says, *"Well, I've never experienced this, therefore I can't experience that."* It's the Reticular Activating System of your brain. Has anybody ever heard of that before? Reticular Activating System is in your left brain, it's your egoist mind and it keeps your sanity. It's a gift from God to you, but the purpose of it is so that Mom, when she's outside and there's seventy kids on the playground and she hears her kid say *"Momma!"*, that part of her brain picks that one voice out of seventy kids that are all saying momma; and it tells her, that's my kid that just said Momma. It's the part of you that seeks the familiar. It's the part of you that defaults back to the familiar. It's meant to keep you on track but because we are sinful beings and have had failures in our life and self-esteem issues, our self-talk often times is negative. When we have these attacks and go through the troubles that we've gone through often times, our self-talk defaults to the negative of our past.

Even though we're in church and trying to renew our mind and telling ourselves, *"I'm a new creature in Christ Jesus,"* our Reticular Activating System, our ego, the ego of our left brain, analytically says that you've never overcome anything before, you've never been anything, this is who you are, and this is how you will always be. It's a lie, it's a fact maybe, but the truth trumps the fact. It's why you've got to renew your mind. You've got to have positive self-talk. You've got to picture yourself as the overcomer that God says that you are.

This seems to happen more often with young women who have self-esteem issues, self-confidence issues; maybe have gone through abuse or something tragic in their life. What happens is that because those women don't feel much self-worth, you can take them, put them in a room of 200 guys that they don't know, and within five minutes the egoist mind, the Reticular Activating System, tells them that they're not worth anything and everyone in the room knows it. It echoes with, *"I'm not good, I'm not a good person"* and pushes that woman to seek out the biggest loser in the room. That ego hones in like a missile asking where to find the loser. Where can I find the loser? Where is he, who is he, who is he? I want a guy without a job. I want a guy that's addicted. I want a guy that will beat me down. Where is he, where is he? Now, that happens all on a subconscious level but it happens just the same. The sad thing is that not only have we seen it, we all know people who don't see their self the way God sees them. They don't want to pick a loser. I don't call the guy a loser, but the fact that he's on the couch, won't work, he's addicted and he's abusive, society calls him a loser. Okay, you get that right? I'm not calling anybody a loser. Don't write me letters or send me emails! You know that loser? I want him in church. I can help him. I've got to renew his mind too, but I'm also working on the young lady that sees herself as worthless.

I want you to hear something young woman. I don't care what you've been through, what hurt you've gone through, you are a precious gem before the Lord. You are so valuable; you are so honorable and therefore you are so worthy of God's best. Woman, you need a man that'll kiss the ground you walk on, that'll serve you, that'll do stuff for you. That's who you are! You need a guy that'll just love you to pieces, just love you! That's what you need! You're worthy of that. Why? Because you're God's daughter, you're God's kid. And what you need to begin saying to yourself is this: *"I am a winner. I am a champion. I am an overcomer. I am a conqueror."*

Psalms 18:28 God illuminates the darkness around me. Indeed with your help God, I can charge an army, by God's power I can jump over a wall.

The King James says it this way: *I can run through a troop and leap over a wall.*

There was a song back in the 70's that said, *"I can run through a troop and leap over a wall, hallelujah, hallelujah."* And we would do that during the song. I can run through a troop and leap over a wall, hallelujah, hallelujah. That song was based on this scripture, but here's the point of that verse; it's that with God's help I can overcome anything. I can conquer an army. I can go over a wall. Whatever opposition is in front of me, if I have hit a wall in my life, I can overcome it.

Maybe you are hitting a wall in your life right now? I want you to know something; you can make it over the wall. An army's coming against you in your life right now. Whether it's a doctor's report, a layoff, a pink slip, a divorce, whatever you're going through, the good news for you is this: **You can overcome it**. How? Through God! Don't you love it?

Philippians 4:13 I can do all this through him who gives me strength.

Whatever I have, Paul says, wherever I am, I can make it through anything with the one who makes me who I am. I want you to know something. You can make it through whatever you go through, whatever opposition, whatever adversity you go through. You can make it and you will make it. That's who you are, wherever you are. Don't be all stressed out and nervous. Learn to let go of control. You don't have to control life. You don't have to control everything.

Wherever I am, I'm home for the moment. I'm nowhere else, I'm here and this is home. Wherever I hang my hat is home. I can make it. You can make it! You will never be able to control everything so just go ahead and let go, breathe and then breathe deeper. God is the one who made you. Don't let any unwholesome talk come out of your mouth. Listen to what God's saying to you. He's saying that you control what you say and think. Don't let any of this self-deprecating, *"I'll never make it, I never get a break, it doesn't work out, why's God doing it for them, but not me"* stuff come out of your mouth or even enter your mind.

That's what God means by unwholesome. Don't do that.

Be Habitual

Another stellar habit that sometimes Christians don't want to hear about is reading the Bible. It's so spiritual though. I'm telling you the success of your life is dependent on it. God lays it out before you in written form, your life and death, blessing and cursing. Choose life. You have other habits as well; traditions, obsessive compulsive actions that you complete daily. You have paths, options, opportunities; the sum total of the success or failure of your life is based, not on one lucky break you get in your decade, but it is based on the daily habits that you have. You have an input into the output. Based on your faith and based on the discipline you are disciples, it means in the Latin, a disciplined one, that's who you are. It's what you do daily, how you eat, how you live, how you think, how you manage your thoughts, what food you put in. What conversations, what talk comes in and out of your mouth? What are you going to do? Great habits equal a great life, I'm just telling you it does. Develop your habits and take pride in them. Don't be ashamed to declare yourself as a person with stellar habits.

Deuteronomy 28:63 Just as it pleased the LORD to make you prosper and increase in number,

The Lord is happy to make you successful and to help your nation grow as you conquer the land. Don't ever stop the testing of your faith, being on the field, practicing in the gym, shooting the free throws when nobody's around, practice the habit of reading God's word, the habit of praying, the habit of coming to church even when you don't feel good. Tell yourself, *"Even when I'm tired and worn out, even when I'm offended and mad at somebody, I'm coming to church. I'm going to shoot the free throws, I'm going to shoot the free throws, I'm going to shoot the free throws; I'm going to shoot the free throws. I'm going to practice. I'm going to live. I'm going to do. Even when there's no glory, even when nobody's applauding me, even when no one's patting me on the back, I'm doing the practice daily, day in, day out. I'll be at my post, I'll arrive on time, I'll arrive early, I'll serve with a smile on my face, nobody's applauding me, nobody's patting me on the back, but I'm going to do it anyway."*

Remember, payday comes, payday comes! G-I-T-H, Get in the Game, be a spectator no longer. Christianity, by the way, is not a spectator sport. It is a player sport. You're in the game.

1 Peter 1:6 says, *for a little while you had to suffer through these trials, but I want you to know, these have come so that your faith, which is of greater value than gold or silver, which perishes when refined by fire, may prove genuine; so that your faith may prove*

genuine and may result in praise, glory and honor when Jesus is revealed. What is that saying? It is reminding you that that payday's coming for your faith. The fact that you stuck to it, that you didn't quit, that when you had the opportunity because you were hurt, because you were offended, because things didn't go well, because nobody patted you on the back, you continued serving God. You're in the race for the long haul. It is not a sprint; it is a marathon.

Keep a strong heart and an enduring spirit for the ability to overcome the biggest obstacle that your mind will face and that is doubt. This won't be easy. We are creatures with feelings and hurt feelings can be one of the most devastating trials because we can't control them. How you can manage those feelings is with your self-talk. Defeat your doubts. Doubts come at all of us. The Book of James says be merciful to those who are fighting through doubt. Don't be rough on them. If you doubt yourself and are having a hard time, remember that the body of Christ is there to help you. I understand your doubts, I've had doubts, but the truth is that you will win. You're going to overcome. You're a champion. You're going to make it. Fight those doubts.

Psalm 27:14 Be strong, take heart and wait for the Lord!

Another verse tells us to put on the full armor of God, to be ready. So come on, put it on, and suit up! To support you during battle, you have to increase your faith. The Bible tells us that every person is given a measure of faith, everybody's got a muscle, but it's up to you to develop your muscle. I want to encourage you, children of God, conquerors of God, conquerors *for* God, overcomers, winners, let me encourage you to become students of the game of life. Become a student. If you're going to be great golfer, you have to become a student of golf. If you're going to be a great football player, a great baseball player, you have to learn the game, to study the game, to study the greats who have played before you. Abraham, Paul and David are the greats that have shined in outstanding performances of their faith. It's your job to study them and become a student of the game of life. Get in the game! Serve God, participate, and run your race you champion! That's who you are, you're a champion. Everything is possible to him who believes, and you're a believer.

1 John 5:4, whatever is born of God overcomes the world and this is the victory that has overcome the world.

How do you overcome all of this opposition, how do you become this person that God says that you are? Your faith, that's how. Who is the one who overcomes the world? ***The overcomer is he who believes that Jesus Christ is the Son of God.***

Chapter 2
Heart Trumps Talent

Don't walk through life just playing football. Don't walk through life just being an athlete. Athletics will fade. Character and integrity and really making an impact on someone's life, that's the ultimate vision, that's the ultimate goal - bottom line. -Ray Lewis

I am writing Overcoming: Overwhelmed because I believe and know that God views you and sees you as an overcomer. Yes, YOU! He sees you as a champion, as a winner. That's who you are. Now, you may not feel that way sometimes. You may have some history in your life that says otherwise. I want you to know something that you may not have ever thought of. You are who God says that you are. That's who you really are, and that's the essence of who you are. So today I want to challenge you to see yourself as a winner, as a champion and as a person that God has created. He made you so that you can do something awesome with your life.

In the last chapter, we looked at the profile of an overcomer and asked ourselves: what does an overcomer look like? This chapter, we're going to look at one aspect out of that profile and learn why Heart Trumps Talent Every Time. The reason I say that is because we often look at talent and skill sets, we look at giftedness and we say "Wow, cool!" But I want you to know something…there's something more powerful than talent. Passion!

Romans 8:37 says this: *amid all of these things, amid all of these problems, amid all of the opposition, amid all the things that all of us go through in life, amid all of these things, we are more than conquerors in Christ Jesus.*

In this verse, Paul is talking to the church and he is reminding you that YOU have victory through your relationship with him. And so I say to you today, you are a conqueror. You are a winner. That's who you are, period. My prayer for you is that you see yourself that way and that today your heart and passion expands. As you view yourself as an overcomer your energy will increase and you will become more of who God has already anointed you to be. If you've read Proverbs 31 before then you know of the Proverbs 31 woman. She is the one that we all want to be like. Even guys want to be like this.

Proverbs 31:16 says that she picks out a field and she buys it. She plants a vineyard from the profits she has earned; she puts on strength like a belt and goes to work with energy. Come on somebody! She sees that she's making a good profit and so her lamp burns late into the night. What a woman! I want to be like that don't you?

The part of the verse that says 'she puts on strength like a belt and she's full of energy' is what I want you to have. What I know about your life is this: If you've got passion and if you've got the strength and the energy, then you can live your life and you can be who God created you to be. If you're tired and worn out feeling depleted and beat up; if you feel like your battles have been too intense and it's too much then rest for a day, but you've got to get back up and you've got to go at it again.

So where does this come from? I want to give you the key to it. I want you to be that person that straps on energy every morning and gets up with purpose and a giddy-up in your step. I want you to want to go somewhere, but how do you do it? Well I'm going to share that with you.

1 John 5:4 Whomever, whatever is born of God overcomes the world.

This is the victory that overcomes the world, our faith. Faith…so what is it? Faith is going to give you the energy to be an overcomer. Hebrews 11:1 says this, *faith is the substance of things hoped for, the evidence of the things that are not seen.* It's the substance, so there's something to it. What is faith? Because if the key to overcoming your problems and overcoming this life is your faith, how do you know exactly "what faith is?"

Faith is the substance of things that you're hoping for, the evidence of the things that you don't see yet. You don't have to have faith to have a chair. You've got a chair and you're sitting in the chair.

You're not believing in God for a chair because you can see the chair and you're in the chair. You might need a new car, you might need a stronger marriage, you might need a better job, you might need a new house and you might need a raise, right? And so I want to encourage you today to have faith for something because if you have faith for it and you see a picture of it, you're going after it, then the energy comes from that. See, here's what I know, the "why" behind what you do is more important than the "how." This is the message, "Heart Trumps Talent Every Time," this is the why behind what you do.

I was watching a football game once and the underdog team, the Ravens, won the game. After the game I heard Ray Lewis say something. He said, *"I love to listen to what they say we can't do, come on tell me what I can't do because when you tell me what I can't do, then I'm going to go do it."* I love the way that sports can relate to preaching about life, like in this instance. I appreciate what Lewis had to say because it speaks of heart, and that speaks of passion. On that same day, the San Francisco 49ers was not the team chosen to be the winners and yet they came back as the underdogs. Let me tell you a little bit about their quarterback. Their quarterback was supposed to be on the bench, and the first string quarterback at the beginning of the year got hurt. So their quarterback stepped up as the underdog on the underdog team. He stood up as the underdog, the one that doesn't have as much talent, the one that was told to sit the bench, to get the splinters in his rear and held his head and his heart high and won that game.

If the bench sitters get an opportunity to step up, often times because of the heart on the inside of them, then they will excel and do more than the first string, the ones with all the talent and skill but no heart. So if you feel inferior or inadequate, if you feel like you are not good enough, remember that you're in good company. That same player on the 49ers, the quarterback, broke every record in the NFL in the history of the NFL in quarterback rushing. Not just in playoff games, but in all games, the guy was psycho. Well how did it happen? Heart! Passion! I want to help find your why and your reason. Your heart has to come from somewhere.

This chapter is about helping you find your why. When you find your why, you get the energy that comes with it. Think of it this way: I take a couple of five gallon paint buckets and set them up on separate sides of a stage. Then I take a ten inch board, a ten inch plank that's thirty feet long and I set it on top of the five gallon buckets. Next I take $20.00 bills from in my pocket, and I pull them out and I say "Hey, I'll give a $20.00 bill to every person that will walk from one end to the other." Would you do it? Are you scared that the buckets would not hold you? So if you are scared, what if I take the buckets out and I just lay the board on the ground? Now how many of you are takers? Pretty much everyone reading this would take that deal.

Now I go to downtown St. Louis and go up to the highest skyscrapers that are equal height and I take that same board, put it across and offer you $20.00. Would you do it? Do you need that $20.00? I guess it just depends on how bad you need $20.00. Ninety nine percent of most people were eliminated when I added the skyscraper because the risk and the danger are too great for us, especially when we feel like there is a minimal reward. The perceived risk is too high.

Let's throw something in to confuse it a little bit more, to create a little bit more thinking. Now on this building, you have a two year old little baby girl. That baby girl is your baby girl and she is on that building. Now that same building is on fire and it is burning. Your baby is on top of that building. Now how many of you are going? You wouldn't do it for $20.00, but you would do it for your baby. In fact, let me turn the situation around even more. You'd pay me $50,000.00 to let you run across to get your baby because at that point it's *your baby*! And what I want to say to you is this; if you're an overcomer and you're going to be the overcomer that God says that you are, you can't just say well, I want the $20.00 reward.

You have to have a "why" that's the same kind of a "why" as what you would do for your own baby. So it's heart and it's passion! How do you get it? Your "why" could be that you have this list of things that you want to do. You want to make a difference in your life. You want to be respected and at the end of your life. You want your children to respect you. You want to make a difference. You want to be a giver and to be a part of funding the kingdom of God. You may say to yourself, *"God I want to build a business, not so that I can get, get, get! I want to build this business and I want millions to flow through my hands so that, **so that**, so that I can fund the kingdom of God. I want to give more, I want to be more."*

What is your why? If your why is not the right why, when the opposition comes you'll sit the bench or you'll give up. If your why and your reason is the right why and reason, you'll go through anything that you have to go through because it does not matter. The thing is not about the thing, it's about you getting to the vision of where you're going. So you need to have a big enough "why" to fuel your energy. Back in the Old Testament, in Ezra, they were rebuilding the temple that had been torn down. It says *that the king should know that we went to the construction site of the temple of the great god of the providence of Judah. It is being rebuilt with specially prepared stones and timber being laid into its walls.* The work going forward is going forward with great energy and great success. What I want you to receive into your life right now is energy and success, but I want to share with you how to get the passion, the heart, the drive, and the "umph" to live your life.

Here are some steps that you can take to see the "how to." All of us have "how to's." For example, there are a lot of "how to's" for becoming a millionaire. You can buy real estate, sell real estate, start a business or you can invent a product or an idea. There are a lot of ways but what makes the difference is the "why" behind the "how to." So these "how to's" that I am going to share with you are packed full of the "why" behind why God has put you on planet Earth.

Step 1: Ask And Ye Shall Receive (The Picture)

The first thing that I want to encourage you to do is to ask God to give you a picture. *"God, I ask you today to give us a picture of our future, to give us a picture of where you want us to go, to see what you've laid out for us."* Maybe you don't know what that picture should be. Because a lot of times you are going through life and asking and you just don't know. You may say, *"I just get up and if I make it then that's great. I'm just trying to get through the day*

Pastor, I'm not even thinking about what I'm supposed to be doing." That's a sad way to live. We've all lived that way before at certain times in our lives. What makes it sad is that we're going through life, just tip toeing through, hoping to arrive safely into the next day.

That's no way to live because God has great plans for you, he has great plans for your life and he wants you to live. Don't just go through life. LIVE it! Now, you will face opposition and there will be some obstacles that you will come up against in your life, but when you have a strong "why" and you have a picture of where you're going, what God has called you to do and who you are, then the essence of His life will bloom in yours. You will go through whatever you have to go through.

If you don't know right now what your picture is, then my encouragement for you to ask God, *"God give me a picture, what do you want for me over this next year? The next five years God? Maybe even the next ten years God... God what do you want me to do? What do you want to do in me? What do you want to do through me God?"* God will give you a picture if you ask him and listen with an open mind. James 1:5 says that if you want to know what God wants you to do, ask Him and he will gladly tell you, for he's always ready to give in a bountiful supply of wisdom to all who ask. But when you ask him, be sure you really expect him to tell and that you are ready to listen. Because a lot of us go *"God what do you want me to do"* and then we go back and we didn't really expect him to tell us.

Be ready, be ready, be ready! If God's going to be involved, then it's going to be so big that you can't do it without Him.

God excels in taking weak vessels and doing awesome and mighty things in them. He excels in taking underdogs and making them winners and champions. So often times you take an underdog, a person who has a bad history, a bad past and maybe they feel inferior. Then God shows them this big vision, an amazing plan for their life. Even though they have seen that picture, a lot of times their self-talk eliminates them because they automatically think "no way, not me. Lord, who are you talking to? It can't be me." What I want to say to you is that when God gives you a picture, you better be ready. Even if it's bigger than you, more massive than your mind can conceive, know this: that's the way God operates and that's the way that God gets his glory. Ask him, *"Lord show me."* Habakkuk says, *read the vision, write the vision, make a plan so that everybody that reads it can run with it.* I want you to look and to ask, not just haphazardly. I want you to pray this prayer this year, starting now. Pray and say *"God what do you want to do, show me the big picture, let me see the big picture."*

You have to receive the picture by faith. Aha! This is where the faith comes in! When God shows you this great thing, do not think to yourself that God sent the wrong email to you. Do not think that that email was intended for someone else. I want to challenge you to see the picture and receive the picture. So when you receive the picture, and you look at the picture, it's okay to say, *"all right, you do know Lord it's going to have to be mostly you. I don't have the talent and*

the skill set and the goodies, but the Lord says I'm going to give you the heart and the Lord gets more glory from your heart than he does your talent." Oh he gets more glory from that! So you need to receive it. Psalms 73:16 says, *when I tried to figure it all out all I got was a splitting headache until I entered the sanctuary of God and then I saw the whole picture.* What that verse means to me is that when I try to plan my life on my own, with my skill sets and my own dreams and my own desires, I get a headache because I know my limitations. I know where I'm limited. I know what I can't do on my own. But when you enter the sanctuary it is symbolic of your fellowship with him, your communion with him. It is when you commune with God, when you connect with God, when you interact with him, not in the religious way, but in a relationship way. *"I had a headache trying to figure this out, but being with you Jesus and getting the picture, I'm getting a picture."*

Step 2: Finish What You Haven't Started

The second step is a bit more complicated, but once you have seen the picture, your next step is to finish it and then start it. That makes no sense really, does it? Finish it then start it? Well it doesn't make sense unless you understand the way things work. Everything works this way. Before the foundations of the world were laid, God finished it. He decided long before he created you and loved you, that even though you were messed up that he would love you, choose you, die for you and call you righteous before you were in behavior. Kind of like whatever building or place that you're sitting in right now. There was a day that people sat down and decided to build the building you are in or the park that you are sitting in, the car that you are riding in. Big circles were drawn; someone drew the big circles and the circles didn't represent people, they represented rooms or trees and the designer said, *"Let's draw this circle"* and drew a circle and decided to put one room here, one tree there, one wheel on the back. Then that designer may have flip-flopped ideas, moved hallways and made rooms, suggested bathrooms and benches, and did all of that on a bubble diagram, then the bubble diagram went to the architect and the architect put his brains to it. The architect decides, okay you need this kind of steel, you need these kinds of anchors to support this load and to do this, we're going to have hallways that are this way, sidewalks here, motors there. We're going to have a ramp here, we're going to do this, put an elevator in. Someone did all of that on paper. It was done and finished on paper before the ground was even broken, before the gas was in the engine.

Oh and let me tell you, that is the way life works too, along the way you get to make adjustments. The picture is already finished. You can see the finished picture and now it's up to you to say, *"Oh I want that. I want to add this."* You know the cool thing about your picture is that you can change it; scribble off something. I've discovered in my own life that there are times that I go after something and once I get it I realize I've wasted too much time on that particular thing and it's not worth it, it wasn't worth it. There are times in life where you realize that something is not as important as you may have thought it was. Maturity has brought a different perspective and has caused you to change your viewpoint.

Sometimes God will show you a picture of what can be, and then as you do life, you will discover that God always takes a picture of what could be, and he makes it better than you've dreamed of or than you've even asked of him. God wants to work in you, He wants to anoint you, and He wants to give you the life that you dream of. He wants to give you a life that is even better than the one that you dream of. So receive it and finish it.

I'd like to tell you about a man named Audie Murphy. Audie Murphy was a famous World War II hero. He received every Medal of Honor that our United States can give out, as well as medals from Belgium and France. Let me give you a little background on Audie Murphy. Audie Murphy was a short, wee, little man like Zacchaeus. A little bitty man; 5'5", small in stature and to look at him you would not see a warrior.

Audie Murphy was turned down from the Marines; he wanted to be a big, bad Marine. The Marines looked at him and said, no thanks, you just, you just…you're not our people. He left and he went to the Navy and the Navy turned him down. He went to the Army, the Army turned him down. He went to the Air Force, and the Air Force did not see use for him. He was turned down by all branches of the military. Audie lost his dad when he was just a boy. His dad left the family and left them alone. He quit school early and went to work. His mother died when he was 17. Audie wanted to be in the military so badly that he just kept trying. Finally, the Army said we'll take him but we'll make a cook out of him. He said, *"I don't want to be a cook. I've got the heart of warrior! I want to be a warrior, a fighter!"* His soul was screaming, *"I'm a fighter!"* No one believed in him, but he believed in the picture that he saw for himself within his heart.

Audie Murphy was the man who single-handedly captured a whole German battalion. He jumped on an abandoned, burning tank while he was out of ammunition and on his own, and he began to overtake the enemy until he captured all of them. He was awarded all of these honors and then he went on to become a movie star. Initially, he starred as himself in the movie that he wrote about his life. He was involved in forty different movies. A wee little man with not much skill, you would think, but because of his passion and his heart it appears that he had all kinds of talent. What I want to say to you is that your heart can trump the talent. You can excel in life; you can become awesome because you've got the goodies on the inside of you.

Step 3: Feed ME!

So now you see the picture. You have finished the picture, but in order to continue on the path that God has planned for you, you have to jump in whole-heartedly and attack step number three. Feed your faith, feed it, and then feed it some more. I challenge you as I read this verse to open your heart and to open your mind to receive it.

Isaiah 43:18 Forget about what has happened, don't keep going over old history, be alert, be present, live in the moment, I'm about to do something brand new, it's bursting out, don't you see it? There it is, I'm making a road in the desert, rivers in the badlands.

You may already be saying, *"But you don't know what I've been through."* Yes, you've been through the same thing everybody else has been through and is going through. Everybody's got their story, everybody's got their opposition. It's just a different name, a different day, a different kind of opposition, but we're all in this thing called the human race. Misery loves company, and we're in good company together. We've all got our story. What I want to say to you is this; prophetically and by the word of God, listen to the encouraging word of God. Quit going over the regrets of your past. Quit beating yourself up with what used to be, the failures of the past and how you got passed over or how people have done you wrong. This is a new day.

God is doing a new thing, can't you see it? Open it up! Open your eyes and look for it! God's doing a new thing and it's for you. That's the hard part because some of us are so focused on our circumstances and our situation that it's all we can see and God's right here going, *"Uh dude? I'm right here; I've got some new stuff going on!"* And you're going on and on about the circumstances! Let go! Let go of the past. Let go of the failure and look for God. Feed your faith. Feed your faith!

Philippians 2:12 says *keep on doing what you've done from the beginning, live in response of obedience.* He's saying that these guys started out in obedience, obedience to God, and he is saying that even when you feel separated from him, keep up. Better yet, double your efforts! Put some more strength into it. Be energetic in your life of salvation; reverent and sensitive before God. The energy that's in you is God's energy and it's an energy that is deep within you. It's called heart. God himself is willing and working at what will give him the most pleasure. *"Wait a minute God! This is about my pleasure!"* You might say. If you really want to get this thing right, if you really want to be an overcomer, it's not about your pleasure because your pleasure is all about me. It is selfish, myself is self-centered. Myself is all about give me, give me, give me, give me, give me, give me, give me. If you really want to get the energy from God, if you want to get the passion and the drive from God, to be effective, to be an overcomer then you say *"God this is about your picture."* Why'd he put you here? So you can live selfishly? No! It is so that you can be effective… an effective partner and an effective co-laborer with Jesus. So your business is not to live a gravy lifestyle. You will get to live a good life, but the purpose of your business is to have more than enough so that you can be a blessing to the kingdom.

The reason He wants you to have a good marriage is so that your marriage can be a blessing, so that you're not focused on the struggles but you're focused on the people around you. See, God wants to bless you but not for you to go off in a corner and just play with your toys. He wants you to get your toys and go share your toys, right? Blessed to be a blessing! Feed it…feed it through gratitude.

Chapter 3
Heart Trumps Talent Even More

"Life is a lot like surfing... When you get caught in the impact zone, you've got to just get back up. Because you never know what may be over the next wave."- Bethany Hamilton, Soul Surfer

Step 4: Be a Righteous Thanker, Dude

Let's do a little sidetrack. This will help you, and this is free. I should charge extra for this, but I won't. You know how sometimes we focus on faith and it's the substance of things hoped for and we want it. We don't have it yet but we're believing for it; the picture that God has for you. You are saying, *"God, I'm believing for this increase, that increase, better marriage, better children, better, better, better"* and you are making your requests known to God, with thanksgiving and gratitude. Why does God want to do that? Here's why, because if there is no gratitude, if you don't thank him, then you are not recognizing what he has done. And all of your mental energy goes into what you don't have yet. Then you are set up because you are not living with content and you are not grateful. Soon you are saying, *"Hey! They got that, I didn't get mine."* Next the enemy begins to play the fiddle in your life and begins to say *"Yeah He's mad at you! Yeah your sins are separating you from receiving the blessings of God."*

It's kind of like this: Did you ever go car shopping and you look at a car that you've never seen before. Suddenly everywhere you look you see that car driving down the road all the time, in all sorts of colors. How did you never notice that before? Why? You are now aware of it. You never noticed it before, but now that you're aware of it, you notice. If all you focus on is what you don't have, then it is so easy to become ungrateful. It's healthy to stop and to live a default gratitude life where you are constantly aware of what He did, the good things He did for you over these last decades and how good He's been. You can begin to mix in how good He's been with what you are believing for now, making it easier to live a balanced life.

As you live with an attitude of gratitude and thankfulness it will help you to watch and live in the moment. You won't be going *"Oh someday I'll be happy when...*" No, you will be happy now because you know that God has been good to you and yeah, it's going to get even better. But oh he's good; that's why we need to be grateful. Protect the vision. Philippians 3:15 says, "*Let's focus on the goal, look at it, focus on it, those of us that want everything God has for us.*" Do you want everything God has for you? The Bible makes it very clear that He has a lot of stuff prepared for you, but you have to go get it. Focus, those of us that want everything God has for us; if any of you have something else in mind, something less than a total commitment, God will clear your blurred vision so that you can see it. I love the verse in Proverbs that says, "*The aspirations, the goals in other words, the aspirations, the hopes, the desires of good people will end in celebration.*" Oh yeah, it's going to be a party!

Here's what I want you to do: through your faith I want you to go ahead and receive it early and start partying now. How can you do that? Well because you learn to look over the past and not to be regretful of it, but to look over the past and to say, "*God, you've been good to me. You helped me through the car accident, through the divorce, through the bankruptcy, through the things that I went through. You helped me make it God, you're good. Now I'm looking forward and I've got great aspirations for what you want to do in my life.*" Now faith says to celebrate early.

So YOU are in the middle of a celebration. Celebrating the victory of your life right now; early and in advance because you know the outcome of your life, you are good people. Not because you've been good; because you haven't and I haven't either. You are good people because you are the righteousness of God in Christ Jesus and He has made you righteous. You're righteous! You may not feel righteous. You may think that there is no way that you can be good enough. You're just righteous because he put it on you. The theological term is he *imputed* it to you. I want you to remember that word; *he imputed righteousness to you.* You're righteous because you've been imputed. You're righteous; I know the outcome, you're righteous, you're a victor.

I'm overwhelmed, you're victorious! You've been imputed with his righteousness.

Step 5: Be At Home in Your Purpose

Be at home in your purpose, because we're not all the same. We're not all called to do the same thing, to be the same thing. The picture is going to look a little bit different for each of us, it says some will be farmers and others will be shepherds; but here's the good news, those that are tired and worn out, you're going to find new life and energy. When you sleep, you will wake up refreshed. Come on! How many of you want to sleep well and wake up ready to face the world and the energy? This is your year!

In the Andes Mountains there's a story of two villages. One that was located in the low land, the other was up on the mountains. The villagers that lived in the low lands never ever climbed the mountain because their enemies were in the mountains above. Every time they would start to dream about climbing, imagining that they were going to conquer the mountain, if they would even attempt it, they would be squashed and stopped. One day, the villagers from up above came down the mountain and they pillaged the village people from the lowlands and they stole and plundered their things and they took one of the Momma's babies. They went back up above into their land and the town's people were grieving and they were hurting. They were sad about losing their stuff, but they were even more upset that they had lost a baby. Because this Momma was special to them, the warriors and the strong men, those with the talent, those with the skills and those with the strength determined that they would climb that mountain and they would go to war to get that Momma's baby back.

And sure enough they did, they climbed the mountain, they tried at least. They attempted it the first time and they failed and so they re-strategized. They developed a different "how to" because the previous one didn't work. Soon they came up with a second, third, fourth, fifth and eventually sixth attempt. They were losing soldiers and they were not gaining any ground. And after the sixth attempt, the strong men from below were huddled in a conference and they unanimously determined to give up because they weren't able to do it. There these warriors are, these yoked out muscle men who had failed six times, and in the middle of their meeting they noticed something. They noticed this woman coming down the mountain holding a baby and it was the baby that they were going after. They stopped her and they said, we, our strongest men we couldn't do it, our plans didn't work, how did you do it? And she looked intently in the eye of these soldiers and warriors and she said it's simple. It wasn't your baby!

Often times we have failed in our plans because we have not allowed God's vision to become our baby. Because I'm going to tell you, there's an enemy out there, there's a thief; just the same as there's a thief on the street that would love to steal your wallet, but there's a thief in your head that would love to steal your dream. He typically tries to steal it through opposition, through problems, through attacks and if you don't own the baby and the baby ain't yours, after four, five, six attempts, you will start to think that it is too hard. But if that dream becomes your baby, if the vision that God shows you, the picture that God shows you becomes your baby, you'll cross the building and you'll do whatever you've got to do because then the thing ain't about the thing. The thing is about your baby.

God has that kind of a vision for every person. Part of my passion in life is to see people like you step out in faith and do seemingly impossible things against all odds and become victorious, especially when in the natural you really don't have the skill sets. When you are that person in the natural that has been through a lot of stuff in the past and should be disqualified yet still comes through with flying colors because, don't tell anybody, you're God's favorite; because you are his baby. What you might have forgotten is that God himself came down the mountain and other people would think *"why would he do that?"* Because he looked at you and he said, *you're my baby*. You're his baby, you're his child and he's crazy for you. This next verse just takes it to a whole new level.

In Matthew 16, Jesus was talking to Peter one day and we know now (2,000 plus years later) that he was really talking to us *through* Peter. The conversation is incredible. God says, *"I'm going to tell you who you really are, you are a rock and on this rock I will put together my church. A church so expansive with energy that not even the gates of hell will be able to keep you out."*

He wasn't talking about your head, he's talking about your heart, and he said I'll take out the stony heart and I'll put in a heart of flesh. What he says about you is *"I'm going to give you so much energy that not even the gates of hell will be able to keep you out."* Now that was good, but this gets even better! Check it out, you will have complete and free access to God's kingdom, keys to open any and every door; no more barriers between you and heaven and earth and earth and heaven. A yes on earth is a yes in heaven. So I hope what you see is that your heart's increasing.

When I was 16 years old I worked at a grocery store. I got a job there the day I turned 16. I'd been working there for about a year and the manager said *"Daren, here is the key to the store and here is the code for the alarm. I want you to open the store tomorrow. At 5:00 in the morning I want you to come in and here's the key."* And I was like, *"I've got the key to Schnucks baby!"* I mean, it felt so good this 17 year old kid with the key to the whole grocery store! And the alarm code on top of that!

The buzz that that gave me just made me feel like I was something. As excited as I was about that, I needed to pull back for just a minute. That is what this verse is telling you. You've got more than the keys to the store and it's not WalMart or Schnucks, and it's not the mall; it's heaven baby! And God is looking at you and he's saying to you and about you; you're the church, you're a rock and on you I'm going to build.

The whole purpose for your business, for your marriage, for your children, for your life is so that you have keys to the kingdom. That's what a God-first life is all about. God has your best interest in mind. Some people are living in fear; they're so *"Oh if I go to God he's going to ask me for all my money, all my time, all my energy."* Well yeah, he is! But he's not going to take it from you, he's going to multiply it back to you, so that you have more friends, more family, in this world he said I'm going to give you, whatever you give up for me, I'll give it back to you thirty, sixty and a hundred fold. That's just good stuff! That is a reason to live life full on! Savor the moment, live in the moment. If you're not living in regret and you've got thankfulness going on, you've got some dreams. Your dreams excite you, by the way, and give you energy. If you've got the energy and the fuel about what you're believing for and you're grateful, then you savor every moment. Savor it, live it, full on!

Step 6: Right is Wrong

Make right the wrong. If you are living wrong or you've got some priorities out of whack, make it right, you can make it right. Listen to this verse in Haggai; people had their priorities backwards and God gave them the chance to repent. In Chapter 1 verse 9 it says: *you've had great ambition for yourself. You've had great dreams for yourself, but nothing has come of it.*

The little that you have gets blown away and there's nothing to it. Why? You ran around all caught up in taking care of your own house and my house lies in ruins. God is saying to us hey, if you've lived a self-centered life or you've got your priorities backwards; remember just to make God first. And if you do that, I can promise you this; you'll never out give God. Number one, with your time or with your resources, number two, he will take care of you. If he doesn't then none of his word is true. If you trust him with your salvation, you can trust him with your time. If you trust him with your fire insurance, you can trust him with your money, amen?

Step 7: Receive IT

Go ahead and receive your promise. There are over 7,000 promises in the word of God. Go ahead and receive your promise. Two great verses, Malachi 4:2, *"For you, Sun rise, the Sun of righteousness will don on those who honor my name."* Honoring, honoring means putting God first; healing radiant from its wings, you will be bursting with energy like colts frisky and frolicking. Oh where'd all this energy come from? It came from honoring God. You will trample over the wicked there will be nothing but ashes under your feet on that day. One more verse, Ephesians 1:17, Paul said, *"I do more than thank."*

I ask God to give you and make you intelligent; discerning and knowing him personally, your eyes fixed, focused and clear so that you can see exactly what it is that he's calling you to do. Grasp the immensity of his glorious way of life that he has for Christians. Oh, the utter and extravagance of his work in us who trust him. Endless energy, boundless strength, all of this energy issues from Christ, the church, Christ's body, in which he speaks and acts, by which he fills everything with his presence. The word enthusiastic means this *en theos*, in God. God in you gives you the energy, He gives you the picture, and He gives you the life. You're an overcomer, you're an overcomer!

Chapter 4
Happy on Purpose

"A man who won't die for something is not fit to live." Martin Luther King, Jr.

It is time for you to see life with energy, with a new perspective, with a new attitude and really through the filter of who God says that we are and that's what we're looking at in this chapter. Who is it that God says we are? What are we and who are we? Are you a hero like Martin Luther King? He is a man who set a great example for those who are facing opposition in their life as he did. He pushed through, he overcame, and he became a great leader. God had that planned for him; he just had to finish the picture.

I want you to know that we often have a perspective of protection and safety for everything that we value; safety above vision. That's never ever been God's way for you. God never says to stay safe and play it safe. God always says to go for it! He is begging you to get out on the edge, get out on the ledge, get out on the limb and live by faith. Part of learning to become overcomers is about measuring up to *who* God says that we are and *what* God says we are.

1 John 5:4, for whatever is born of God overcomes the world and this is the victory that has overcome the world our faith.
So we're talking about faith again. In the last chapters we have learned what an overcomer looks like and some of the traits of an overcomer. We learned about passion and how you get the "why." The "why" of what you do is not about how you become an overcomer, but instead it's the "why" of why you are an overcomer. You'll find the "why" as you discover *your* why.

Now we are going to talk about your mindset and we will learn about that mindset by studying other people who overcome.

Specifically, I want to talk to you about the mindset of happy. Do you know that it is okay for you to want to be happy? I met a woman one time that divorced her husband because she said she wasn't happy. Well that doesn't qualify as a reason for divorce. I'm going to teach you how to be happy in prison. And if your marriage is a prison, I'll teach you how to be happy in it. How do you have a healthy perspective, a healthy mindset? How do you get this?

I was watching the NFL playoffs last week and I watched one of the guys on the losing team after the game, and I was just was amazed at what his perspective was. He said that when his team lost the game, he was angry and mad until he got to the end of the tunnel. That meant that he was mad from the time he left the field until he got through the tunnel and then he said that by the time he hit the end of the tunnel he was already thinking about next season. That's the difference between pros and amateurs. A professional has the ability to turn off a bad day, a bad season, a bad game, even a bad year, and say *"next year, next month, next game"* and I want you to know that that is really the prospective you should have as a Christ follower. It is the healthy perspective of saying *"You know what? I may have had a bad day, but there's tomorrow and there's today and I'm getting up today."*

1 Peter 1:13 says to *"prepare your minds for action."* God is saying to the church, to you, to prepare your mind for action. Not for the couch, but for actions, to do something. Proverbs 14:30 says, *a sound mind makes a robust body, but a runaway emotion corrodes the bones.* I want to balance this message with yes; I'm going to teach you how to be happy. I'm also going to teach you how to control your emotions, because if you're like me and most people are pretty much like each other, we've all had those moments in our life where we've let our emotions just run. A circumstance or a situation happens, we get our feelings hurt or we get an opinion about a situation, and we get to feeling strong emotions. It is like driving a car. I want to teach you how to stay in the driver's seat and use your emotions, because the Bible tells us your emotions are a gift from God. Those emotions just need to learn how to ride shotgun.

Happy Happy Happy

Since we're going to talk about happiness and emotions, I want to give you a definition that I came up with that I think kind of describes the word happiness. All of us have a different definition for different words. I don't know what your definition is for the word happiness, for the word happy, but I want to give you the one that I want to use for this message. Here it is: *Happiness is a mental and emotional state of being that creates a feeling of joy and excitement that when you get your internal focus optimistic as you can, imagine the best and move with positive expectation.* That's a mouthful; so read it again.

Happiness is a mental and emotional state of being that creates a feeling of joy and excitement that when you get your internal focus is optimistic as you can, imagine the best and move with positive expectation.

God wants us, you, me, all of us to enjoy our lives, and that's what we're going to talk about. In fact, I'll tell you how important this happy message is. Jesus' first message he ever preached, the Sermon on the Mount in Matthew Chapter five was all about happy, happy, happy, happy, happy... blessed, blessed, blessed. It depends on what translation you read it out of. The Amplified Bible gives the Greek word for happy is blessed; happy to be envied and prosperous is the person who does these things. He said *"Happy are those who* and then he gives a list, He says *happy are those that get to know God. Happy are those that trust God. Happy are those that expect God to meet their needs."* There's that expectation... looking forward with expectation. *"Happy are those that follow God's instructions. Happy are those that cultivate a forgiving spirit. Happy are those that maintain a clear conscience. Happy are those who build healthy relationships. And then the last one he gave us, happy are those who live with an eternal purpose in their mind."*

So Jesus did a whole series on this thing called happy because in that day they could preach a whole series in one message. Those sermons were about eight or nine hours long! Today we don't do that, do we? David wrote in the book of Psalms 37, *"Seek your happiness in the Lord and then the promise is, the counter balance of that is that if you seek your happiness in the Lord he'll give you the desires of your heart."* You've got to know God's will, so how do you know it? You do it by renewing your mind; the battleground is in your mind. You will win or lose this thing of a healthy mindset in your mind. This is because your mindset is your mind, and it's your attitude. How do you win or lose? Well, it's the battle that you face; it's the fight that goes on in your mind and the way you win this fight is to renew your mind.

Romans 12:2, in the Amplified Bible says this, "*Be transformed, changed by the entire renewal of your mind, by its new ideas and by its new attitude.*" You want a new attitude so that you may prove for yourself what the good, acceptable and perfect will of God is; even the thing which is good, acceptable and perfect in his sight for you.

HIT The Refresh Button (RENEW)

"How do I know God, what is your will? What is your will? What is your will? What is your will God? Should I buy this car or that car? Should I go to this school or that school? Should I date this guy or that guy, this girl or that girl? What should I do God?"

He says to renew your mind with its new ideas and with a new attitude, the entire renewal and refreshing of your mind. It's like a detox or a body cleanse. You are going to get rid of the waste so that there is room for all the good stuff to fill you back up. Why do you renew your mind? So that you may find out his will. So that you know what he wants you to do, go right or left.

1 Timothy 6:12 Fight the good fight for the true faith, hold tightly to the eternal life which God has called you, which you have confessed.

Did you know that one of the best things that can happen in your life is when you find your fight? We're so politically correct. We're taught in this country not to fight, not to be controversial; to keep our thoughts and ideas to ourselves. I'm not telling you to go out and physically attack someone, but you need to get a fight on the inside of you. Maybe some of you have never been in a physical fight before and some of you have. Those of you that have, you know that there is an adrenaline rush, there is a high that comes from your fight. It's a buzz and it's scary sometimes, but I want you to know something. I'm not talking about flesh and blood because our fight is not against flesh and blood and it's not against people. What is our fight?

It's this fight to overcome that obnoxious stuff that my mind battles with every day. It's that voice in my head that says, *"Daren, you're never going to amount to anything, Daren you're just average. Daren, you're just mediocre."* It's that self-talk that we mentioned before, it's that left brain ego that tells you that it's okay to calm it down, be cool, chill out; to just be average. You need to find the fight on the inside of you because when you find your fight, you find your energy. When you find your fight you have found your passion. Are you with me? It's not okay to just be. BE alive. BE excited. Fight to BE!

Picture this, God is calling all of you, *"Come on, come on Betty, come on John, come on James, come on Tim, come on!"* You're called! I'm calling you and He's calling your name so hold on and hold tight. You're going to have to fight for it because every obstacle, every circumstance, every doctor's report, every financial report... I mean there's opposition everywhere and then you meet your own worst enemy. YOU! I know that I'm my biggest adversary often times. Dr. Martin Luther King also said this famous quote: *"The ultimate measure of a man is not where he stands in the moment of comfort and convenience."*

Anybody can be groovy when they're comfortable and convenient. You like groovy? Anybody can be groovy when everything's groovy. But during times of challenge and controversy, that's when the ultimate test of a man comes out. That when you find out if you are a real man or if you're a real woman. All hell's breaking loose, things aren't going so well, everything is a mess and God is asking you, *"Have you got your fight on? Can you put the smile on? Can you still remain consistent and can you still remain happy?"*

An Emotional Gift

Our emotions, they're a gift to us from God, they really are. God gave you your emotions. Emotions are not demonic, although they would appear sometimes to be. They are a gift from God that is a part of your soul. Your soul has to be sanctified, which is just a religious term for saying "renew your mind." When you get saved, your spirit gets saved, a perfect spirit; you're perfected in your spirit.

Your body, bad news, it never gets saved! Your flesh, well it is still flesh, but your soul gets renewed and it's called sanctification. It's a process of renewal of the mind. When you study the word, meditate on the word, put this stuff into practice, take control of your emotions and take control of your thoughts...that's called sanctification. It's not a word you use and you won't go to the store and ask to buy a bottle of sanctification.

1 Timothy 6:17 Have faith in God who is rich and blesses us with everything we need"

Everything we need to what? Enjoy life! This was a paradigm shift for me because I grew up thinking that serving God had to be painful and horrible. The more painful and the more horrible it was, the more points I got! Beat me up, step on my toes, tell me how horrible I am, hell fire and damnation, then I was like *"Yeah, I'm right with God now, I've been all beat up."* It was a paradigm shift for me to find out that God really has laid out a path for us to live and to walk in. That he has given us everything we need to enjoy our life. I love that verse.

Deuteronomy 28:63 says *"The Lord is happy to make you successful and to help your nation grow while you conquer the land."* A lot of us don't want to hear the "conquer the land" part. That's the fight. You and I have to go out and conquer the land, multiply, be fruitful, multiply, go out and conquer, dream, have goals, overcome, you're a winner, you're a champion, build that business, build that career, build that marriage and relationship, help your children grow up, get a dream, work in the ministry, get involved in the ministry, get passionate about life. BE!

And when you conquer, I'm telling you that God promises that he will make you successful. I love that verse. Emotions are a gift from God, 1 Corinthians 2:4 says this, *"Stir in the minds of the hearers, you're the hearers, so I'm going to stir in the minds of the hearers, the most holy emotions."*

Your emotions are holy and they are a gift to you from God, persuading them so that your faith might not rest in the wisdom of men, human philosophy, but in the power of God. The temptation, even for Christians, is to go to the wisdom of the world and think that if the world says this; this is how you handle your money, this is how you do this, this is how you do that then maybe you should do it that way too. God says, don't go to the world for your wisdom, no, go to the Lord for his power. His…what's His power? His ability, His ability, God has the ability to take average and turn it into exceptional. God has the ability because of His power to take a dream and make it a reality. God has the ability to help you out. God has the ability to no matter what you're going through and how bleak the report would be, by the economy or by doctors or by any other situation, God has the ability to get all involved and to help you become who he says that you can become.

Chapter 5
Entitled To Be Happy

*"In terms of playing ability there is nothing to choose between
number one and one hundred. Instead, it's a question of who believes
and who wants it more? Which player is mentally stronger? Which
player is going to fight the hardest in the big points? These are the
things that determine who is the champion." -Novak Djokovic*

Winning is an attitude. Success is an attitude. What I'm talking
about is having that attitude, not an entitlement philosophy. That
kind of attitude is so popular today, I'm entitled. Right now it is so
politically correct to give everybody on every team a trophy.
Everyone is a winner. Everyone is the best. The truth is that there's
only one first place, and sometimes your team doesn't get it. Even
in churches when you teach that type of thing, people scratch their
head and don't understand because of the socialism that's entered
our world. Everything's equal, everybody's equal. The truth of the
matter is that some people are successful and some are not.

The Bible even separates winners and losers. God views you as a
winner, God views you as a conqueror, but you have to quit thinking
that it's entitled to you. Here's the balance: you should expect it, but
don't expect it to be just given to you, expect it "when." "When"
what? When you work for it! When you put in the work and the
effort, then you should expect it. When you give your best you
should expect it, but if you are going to sit on the couch all day, then
why should you expect it?

Happy By Default

I want to teach you specifically how to become a student of joy, how
to become a student of success and how to become a student of
happy; a student that is entitled to be happy. In fact, I want to
encourage all of you to make happy your default emotion. Now this
is the key, this is where the nitty-gritty is, because for most of you it
will take a while to stay on track. I still don't have this down all the
way yet. If you do, you come and see me; I'm going to let you write
my next book. But I can promise you this, I am working on this and

I'm going to teach you how I'm working on it and what the scripture has to say.

How do I make happy my default emotion? How do I do that? Well number one, I have to have a plan for happy. And if you don't have a plan for it, it's not going to happen. Things that you don't plan for won't happen. You have to plan. You might accidentally get happy, but I can promise you this, it'll just be because of a circumstance. It won't last very long because there will be another circumstance that comes along right behind that one that's pretty rough. So how do you have happy in good circumstances and keep happy in bad circumstances? Have a plan for happy.

If you're the type of person who wings your life, who just wings it, then you're in trouble. You've got to have a plan. I'll be honest with you, I like winging it because winging it takes responsibility off of me. When I just wing it I'm like, *"Hey you know, whatever, I'm fine."* Here's the problem with winging it: when circumstances happen, you have a default. You have a subconscious default, and when you're winging it you will most likely default to your most familiar and your most common emotion. When things are crazy and the doctor gives you a report and your default is fear, you'll freak, you'll cry, you'll scold the heavens! If you don't have a plan you will default to your most familiar emotion; allowing your circumstances to control you. So you have to have a paradigm shift in our thinking. Here's the paradigm shift; that we can manage and that we can control our emotions.

A lot of us feel like I don't have control over our emotions, they just like whip you around, like the tail on a dog. What was that? That's my emotions whipping me. I understand there's a part of us that sometimes has a chemical imbalance, sometimes it's a medical situation, but what I'm talking about is me and you becoming healthy in our mindset. That's what I'm talking about and we're going to get there. Many of us get addicted to our emotions or we get addicted to feelings of defeat or addicted to feelings of being a victim. Though we would never maybe say that, on a subconscious level, we kind of internally expect to never really be the first place winner. A lot of us never really expect to be the champion, we expect fifth place; we expect to be average, to just be.

Maybe you don't view yourself as a person of excellence. Your self-talk even says to some of you that you are lazy, shy, unorganized, scatter brained, always in debt… those are the type of things that I want to challenge you on. I'm not even saying get legalistic about it. I'm just going to challenge that process of thinking. I want to go there with you, because you have an emotional engine on the inside of you. Vroom, vroom! It's an emotional engine that if you don't train it, and you just wing it and you just let life happen, because of past circumstances, because of abuse, because of addictions, because of things that have happened, maybe because of the environment that you grew up in, we get addicted to certain things and if we're not on our game and when I say on our game, I mean in the word and fighting the fight of faith, then we default to being a victim.

Many of us have even sabotaged our own success. With the crazy odd's that the lottery has, why would you buy a ticket? Let me tell you why you would buy a ticket; because somebody wins! And I know that's why people buy tickets. It's because somebody wins. If nobody ever won, nobody would ever buy them, but because you do hear of people winning from time to time, people buy tickets because there is that chance, there is that hope. But have you heard this statistic? Most often when people do win the lottery, I mean it's up towards ninety percent of the people who win, within five to ten years they are broke again. Do you know why? It's because of this principle; the default principle.

Let me share something with you, if you ever get a million dollars, the first thing you need to do with it is become a millionaire. What does that mean? It means you've got to be a millionaire in your mindset. Because if you get a million dollars and you're not a millionaire in your mind, then your emotional engine will say *"I'm not worthy, I don't deserve this, this is not normal, no it's not normal,"* and your engine will drive you back to what is familiar. Neuroscience calls it your Reticular Activating System, but the word of God says you need your mind renewed. It will take you on a journey and it will drive you right back to broke. This is miserable and I'm comfortable in my misery and some of the truth is that some of us are more comfortable in our misery than we are with happiness.

I want to challenge you, if you are ever going to be the conquerors and the winner and the champion that God says that you can be; do you know what you have to learn to do? You have to learn to be comfortable being uncomfortable. That means that there's a transitional period. It may be a job, the ministry, a million dollars or the business that you're building and your soul is saying to you; *"You're out of place, you're a drug addict, you're out of place, you're an alcoholic, you're out of place, you've been through this, you've been through that, you're out of place, you don't have the smarts, you're out of place, you don't have the faith."* Here's what I'm telling you:

"NO! NO! NO! NO! NO! That's a lie of the enemy!"

You're a new creation altogether in Christ Jesus. You're going to have to renew your mind and remind yourself and remind the enemy who you are. You can do all things through Christ. You're not who you used to be. You're a brand new creature so don't hold onto those things. Don't run on those auto pilot programs of a chip on your shoulder or the defeated "I always lose" mentality. We become so familiar with something that we seek that thing out, no matter if it is good or bad for us. A typical mindset that most people have is that they go on auto pilot to failure, to average or to common and I'm just challenging you to see yourself as more.
I don't see you as average. I don't see you as common...you're uncommon. Why? Because you are followers of Jesus, you're renewing your mind, you have hope, you praise the Lord, you're worshipping and he's doing great things in your heart. If you're going to be an overcomer you're going to have to minimize your abuse. You're going to have to minimize in your mind your old behavior, your old addictions. Minimize them, that's not who you are. Yeah you went through it, and it is part of your story, but it's a minimal part of your story. Because the biggest, best part of your story is yet to come. That's who you are and it is who God wants you to be. So I'm challenging you to renew your mind and renew your thinking.

Proverbs 29:11 A fool expresses all of his emotions, but a wise person controls them.

Did you read that? So, you can control them? Yeah the Bible says you can control them. A wise person does control their emotions.

Habakkuk 3:18 I will be happy with the Lord, I will find true joy in God who saves me. The Lord almighty is my strength, he makes my feet like those of a deer and he makes me walk on the mountains.

I WILL BE Happy And Get To Know God
That verse says "I WILL BE" not "I'm going to try to be" or "someday, maybe I can." It says I WILL BE HAPPY. It's not enough to rest your fate on someday. Someday I'm going to be a good pastor. NO, I'm going to be a good pastor today. I am going to be the best that I can be today. I am the Lord's kid; you are the Lord's kid. Choose happy today. Not everything's going all groovy but be happy today in the middle of it. Sometimes we just need to repent, you know the word repent just means you're going one direction, repent, turn around go a different direction and put God first basically. Job 36 says, *"If you'll obey the Lord he'll make you successful and happy.*

See we lie to our self often times. 1 Peter 3 asks you if you want to be happy. It goes on to say, *"Then stop saying cruel and quiet the telling of lies to yourself."* So the next thing is this, get to know God. Happy are those who know you. Spiritually poor or needy, knowing that you have a need for God, the kingdom of heaven belongs to them. How many of us know our need for God? I can't do this life without him. I can't do happy without him. Happy comes from knowing Jesus. Happy is found in Jesus. Outside of Jesus, at my best, I might hit it occasionally, but in Jesus I can be happy through all things.

Psalm 34:8 "Oh taste and see that the Lord, our God is good, blessed, happy, fortunate to be envied as the man who trusts and takes refuge in him.

I just encourage you to choose happy. Taste God…most of the time we're addicted to what we're familiar with and what we know. You're going to have to just get outside of your comfort zone a little bit and move into the challenge. 1 Thessalonians 5:16 says, *"Be happy in your faith and rejoice and be glad hearted continually, always unceasing in prayer.*"

Now, I want to stop on that verse and share a little bit of science with you, okay? The bible is so scientific and a lot of times science is separated from faith and I don't like doing that. I like bringing science and faith together. I love it because when you study science you really realize that the word was right all along. And neuroscience tells us this that if you're unhappy and if you're depressed, maybe you're in a circumstance or a situation that's just bumming you out, that if you want to break the pattern in your mind, you create a vacuum in your mind by interrupting the emotion that you're experiencing at the moment. Now watch this, this is what the Bible's been telling us all along.

What does the Bible say in the book of Psalms? "*Jump for joy, clap your hands all you people.*"

So you're sitting there, you open the envelope and the bill says you owe way more than what you know you owe and the temptation is to get on the phone like I did the other day and got one of those automated systems. They're nice, but they're automated. It says, "If you would like to pay your bill please say yes." So I say "*No!*" Then the automated lady answers with: "I'm sorry, did you say yes?"

"No, I did not say yes! Give me the operator!" Are you with me? What I'm saying to you is that I need this message probably more than you guys do. So, anyway, I got it worked out. The guy calmed me down; they were overcharging me and I didn't like that! Here's what I know though; when those emotions come and those feelings and the default of unhappy comes, what neuroscience tells us is you do something to create a break in the pattern. Like, for example, have you ever gotten up to go into the other room to do something, and then you forgot what you're there for? Have you ever done that? You walk in there and you're like, what did I come in here for? What did I come in the kitchen for? And so, what happens is when you break the pattern, you create a vacuum in your brain for just a minute. Now here's what the bible says. The bible says jump for joy, shout for joy, clap your hands all you people, lift up holy

hands to the Lord, sing songs, hymns and spiritual songs unto him. How do you get happy?

You stimulate yourself! In Acts it says that you should stimulate, instead of being drunk with alcohol, stimulate, get your buzz from what? Get it from songs, hymns and spiritual psalms. So what these neuroscientists are telling us is that the way you can break the pattern and become happy and have happy be your default is to… you're sitting in your chair, you get a bill like I had, you stand up real quick, you run around the table real quick, you do something crazy, you scream and all of a sudden you break your pattern and you're not quite so upset anymore.

Yes, you might think that sounds subterranean but the word tell us that if we will put God first and instead of focusing on the circumstances lift our hands to God, shout hallelujah, God is good! So let go of control and trust God because so often my own disappointment is this, it's that I'm trying to control everything. So what if I got a bill and it's more than I owe. I can make a phone call and I don't have to lose my mind to do it. I don't have to lose my peace and my joy to do it. I am not paying that bill no matter what. So I might as well keep my happy on, right? I might as well be happy whatever the situation brings. Let go of control.

So you know what you need to do? Maybe this will just help you remember; you need to fire yourself from trying to control everything. Amen? John 16:22 *"You are now very sad, but later Jesus said, when I see you, you will be happy that no one will be able to change the way you feel."* When you make happy your default and you let go of control and it becomes your default emotion instead of anger, resentment, fear, victimization or entitlement. No, what happens is happy is my default. Now it's a process, I told you I don't have it all down yet, but I can promise you this, I'm working on it. That news can come to me and I'm not going to freak out. I mean I've had some pretty rough news come to me over the years and I breathe, and when I breathe I breathe all the way deep down below my belly button and I let go because I know this, I can only do so much anyway, he is the one. And for my faith to work, I have to let go of the control.

You need to pray to God: *God you're in control. If it all ended today, I have no control over that.*

Colossians 1:11 His power will make you patient and strong enough to endure anything, his power will, there's that power again. And you will be truly happy.

Aren't you glad he put that on the end of that verse? He could have left that part off the verse and it would have still been a good verse right? It would have been a good verse all by itself, but then he put that part, "and you'll truly be happy." His power's going to be able to help you make right choices, give you wisdom and make your mindset what it needs to be. You know, make this mindset thing paramount in your life; really it is, relax, relax, relax, let go.

John 16:24 You haven't asked for anything in this way before, but now you ask in my name and it will be given to you so that you'll be made completely happy!

Wait a minute, pray in the name of Jesus? What's the reason for this? Did it really say that? Wait a minute, no, that doesn't seem spiritual enough to me. Here's the advocate of the religious mind, this verse would be more appropriately stated this way, "*you have not asked for anything in thus way before, but now you must ask in my name, then it shall be given to you, so that his name will be made great.*" His name's already great. It says so that you'll be made completely happy. Now I didn't make that verse up, that is right out of the Bible.

Proverbs 3:13 Happy is the man who discovers wisdom and gets knowledge.
See how do you do this? Focus on your reward. See I may be in the middle of some stuff today, but I'm an overcomer and I will get through this. I've overcome before! This is not the end; you've been through some things, five years ago, fifteen years ago, twenty-five years ago, that at the time you thought they would destroy you. Hey, but you're all sitting here tonight and you've got history over your shoulder and I don't know how you got through it and you don't even know how you got through it, but you did and you will get through it again. You're an overcomer and the key is not to quit

on God. You might not get through it the way that you planned, and the how might not be the how that you would pick, but you will because that's his promise, you will get through it.

Focus and meditate.

Hebrews 10:35 So do not throw away your confidence; it will be richly rewarded.

Don't let this happy trust in the Lord die away. No matter what, remember your reward. What's he saying? Don't quit, don't you quit! Remember your reward, remember what's coming! There's an eternity coming, remember that eternity. You will get through it. James 1:2 says, *"Be very happy when you're tested in different ways."* You know that such testing of your faith produces endurance. Endure until your testing is over, then you'll be mature and complete. Then you won't need anything, your needs will be met because you'll have the faith and the maturity to get whatever you need through your faith.

Be Generous

Generosity leads to a happy life. As I was writing this, I studied a bunch of different scriptures and I was amazed at how the word happy and emotional happiness was so related more than any other subject, and it was related to our generosity and our heart of giving. As the pastor of Enjoy Church I had to stop for just a second and realize how generous my church had been. I did not realize it because it's kind of like looking in the mirror, you know how when you look in the mirror you don't see yourself grow, but you're growing. You grow, you know you just don't see it happening until it doesn't fit anymore or the kids you know, you didn't see the kids grow, but they come and they say these shoes don't fit anymore. You don't know what happened, but they don't fit. Anyway, you don't see yourself growing, but I want you to know you don't see what you've done and what you accomplished just the same as I didn't even see what my church had accomplished. So I found my happy and this is what I had to say to my church.

Enjoy Church, this has been a fabulous year for us here. I want to thank you for putting God first. It all started last year at the fast when you guys put God first during that twenty one day fast. It set us up for incredible things to happen and then Easter time we saw dozens and dozens of people come to Christ over our Easter services. We rebuilt the wall outside, being good stewards of our property; we tore down the old building that was outside to make room for new parking and better parking and to clean the area up. We also remodeled our Good Life bookstore. We upgraded all of our equipment. I mean state of the art with scanners and barcode scanners and touchscreens and put couches in there. We even have gift cards available in there. You guys have upgraded the FlashPoint Youth Center, thank you Todd and Rachel and all of the volunteers that have made that happen. Our Satellite Kidz area has been remodeled and painted with beautiful murals. It's incredible!

At our Collinsville campus we've seen many people come to Christ. We started this campus brand new this year. We've upgraded our lighting, our sound and audio equipment is brand new, even our children's rooms have been upgraded with all of the best equipment. It's beautiful, your kids love it. We started our Spanish speaking service reaching the Latin community. Another big accomplishment is we kicked off our Do Something Ministry. Our Do Something Ministry is a multi-faceted ministry that reaches a lot of people that does a lot of different things. Last year we kicked off our emergency response, in fact, we even have a trailer now that's in the back of the building that we're equipping and stocking to keep ready for emergency response. You've ministered at the Salvation Army; you've ministered with Arms of Love and worked with them. Riverbend Headstart, the backpack project for our second year in a row, we've done more than ever this year. We've raised money for coats and bought coats for young children who weren't able to stay warm. Several years in a row that we've done the Shoebox campaign to minister to young children in foreign countries. You've worked with us here, we have a benevolence program where we work together with other churches, it's called CUTS and we meet the needs of families who are hurting. We work with the Community Hope Center reaching our region. Enjoy Church I also want to thank you for what you do to reach hurting people. You've worked with Hands of Hope to dig wells, drinking water for villages in India that didn't have clean fresh drinking water. We've built churches in India with Joyce Meyer. You support orphanages, one in Romania, House of Hope and then again in Haiti we work with Dominic Russo Ministries, all over the world with our own missionaries in Southeast Asia; they work to put an end to sex trade slavery. This year our Tribute to the TSO outreach was incredible. We reached new people and saw dozens and dozens of people come to Jesus Christ as a result of your efforts, your service and your outreach. And then just a few weeks ago, we kicked off our You Got Served campaign. Serving and doing random acts of kindness throughout the community. The list goes on and on and on. I want to thank you for being the type of church that you are, for loving people. This year, I want you to believe with me that we are going to see God do more, reach more people and that your lives are going to fulfill the purpose and the destiny and the plans that God has for you.

I am the pastor of a church of overcomers that is breeding more overcomers. Isaiah chapter 32 says this, *"Happy and fortunate are you who cast your seed upon many waters. When the river overflows its banks for the seed will sink into the mud and when the waters subside the plants will spring up and you will find that after many days you will reap an abundant harvest"*
Are you with me? YOU, who safely send for the ox and the donkey to range freely. I love this verse because it says your happiness is found in your serving and in your giving. I want to challenge you in your giving, always give what you need. If you need more love, give love. If you need more friendship, be a friend to somebody. If you need finances, you need to sow finances. Whatever you need, sow more of that because you always reap what you sow. God wants you happy, would you agree? He wants you to have wisdom, he wants you to be able to control your emotions because your emotions are most holy, and they are a gift from God to you. I hope that I have stirred your emotions to seek God, to put God first in

every area, every aspect of your life and to realize that you are a winner, you're a champion, and you're an overcomer.

Chapter 6
Write It to Right It

"Your time is limited, so don't waste it living someone else's life. Don't be trapped by dogma - which is living with the results of other people's thinking. Don't let the noise of others' opinions drown out your own inner voice. And most important, have the courage to follow your heart and intuition." -Steve Jobs

Overcoming: Overwhelmed is about seeing ourselves the way that God sees us. God sees you as a winner, as a champion and, by the way, God's not mad at you. I grew up thinking that God was mad at me. He's not mad at you, he's for you, not against you and he wants to bless you.

He wants to take you into your destiny and into the purpose that he has for your life. The first chapters talked about the profile of an overcomer, what an overcomer looks like and what character traits they have. What do they do that's different than people who never overcome, who never seem to win? Next we discussed talent. See, there's a lot of great talent in the graveyards today that never was expressed or that never did great things. After that I talked with you about the ability to control and manage your own emotions and making your default emotion that of happiness; wouldn't that be cool if we all lived by that one? Now it's time to talk about the profile of an overcomer that has a strong plan.

God wants you to have a great year this year and my prayer is that your dreams, goals and plans are resurrected. Maybe they've been dead for a while…maybe you've laid them on the floor thinking that it's not going to happen for me. It's never happened before, I've been a dreamer before and I've always been disappointed. Well, I've got news for you! We're going to resurrect those dreams from the dead. I heard a while back from one of my children's church workers that while working with the kids, she asked the children if they knew what the resurrection was. One little boy he raised his hand and he said, "I don't know for sure what it is, but I do know that I was watching on television and they said that if the resurrection lasts for more than four hours you are supposed to go to the emergency room!"

I'm going to resurrect some dreams on the inside of you moving forward. If you continue to do what you've always done, you're going to get what you've always got.

Deuteronomy 12:8 Don't continue to do the things the way we were doing them at the present, each of us doing as we wish, until now you have arrived at your goal, the resting place, the inheritance of God.

God is giving you a blessing. God is giving you an inheritance. God's giving you a destiny and until now you haven't reached it yet.

What he's saying is that maybe you've done some things but you're not there yet. God has a plan and God has a strategy for your life. Today we're going to move into that.

2 Corinthians 10:13 Our goal is to measure up to God's plan for us.

I love that verse because in it He says that our goal is for us to measure up to God's plan for us. I want you to know is that God has a plan for your life. God didn't just create you. God didn't just breathe the spirit life into you and then just say "Hi! You're on your own! Good luck!" No, God has a plan for you, but I also know this, that although God has a plan for you, he has also given you the free will to choose whether or not you take his direction. It is up to you to cooperate with his plan. So my prayer is that we realize that he has a plan and that we begin to cooperate with this plan.

Super achievers have been studied through the years. People like Steve Jobs and Bill Gates, these super achievers of the world, and as they've studied them they found two common denominators. These two traits are so simple and I believe that you can develop them. The first common denominator that one hundred percent of the super achievers in the world have is an unyielding hunger to learn and to grow. That's a great trait to have isn't it? It is an appetite to learn, to increase, to get better, to get more information and to get more knowledge. They've said it this way… readers are leaders.

The second thing that they have in common is that they have clearly written goals, specific plans laid out. And the minute you begin to take and write down your goals, you separate yourself from ninety seven percent of the rest of society because out of a hundred people only three will have some type of a goal and have it written down. Many people say that they've got the dreams in their head. Don't just think it, ink it! Write it down, make a plan.

I heard a story recently of three young Boy Scouts that were hiking in the woods. One day they came out of the woods and they came into a clearing and they looked at this field. They noticed that as they began to walk, that their footsteps made prints in the field from the dew. And so they decided to have a contest. They would see who could walk across the field the fastest and yet make the straightest line. The first young man began to walk carefully putting one foot in front of the other, staring at his feet, and giving all of his attention to his feet.

The second young man followed his lead and had the same result. The third young man looked across the field and saw an oak tree on the other side of the field and as he saw the oak tree he set out toward the oak tree, not giving notice to his feet, but keeping his sights set on the oak tree and the vision before him. As he did this, he tripled their speed at going across the field, but not only did he triple the speed, when he got to the other side, they looked back and they noticed that he walked a straighter line. The others had zig-zagged because they gave all of their attention to every single step.

How does that play out to you? I have talked about this before in this book. You don't just need to have a dream; you need to have a vision, something that inspires the passion in your heart. It is the thing that keeps you going and it and will increase the speed of you receiving it. So, let me help you today to do some things that will help you practically. This is not a deep and real part of the chapter, but more a technical, clinical, practical plan.

First, you have to build a life plan. What does that mean; a life plan? A life plan means this: before you make dreams and goals you need to decide what kind of a life you're going to live. What's valuable to you? What do you value most? For all of us we should have two things besides the two things that we said we had a desire to grow. We should have two higher goals that are higher than anything. The first is to live a God-first life. I strive to lead people to enjoy and experience a God-first life. That ought to be a common denominator of every single person reading this book. You need to have a desire to say that God's first. God wants to be involved all in your career, marriage, family, hobbies, recreation and everything else that you do. Whether it's playing cards or going to a Cards (Cardinals) game, doing whatever you do; God is the centerpiece of it all because you live a God-first life number one.

Secondly, you should also have the desire to make love your greatest aim. Now those are the two common denominators, but I'm going to get real practical with you for just a few minutes. How do you set goals for your life and how do you really make them obtainable? First of all, design your life. What do you want, what do you value? This will be different for everyone; those two were the same. For example, what's valuable to you? Do you want to eat at home every night with your family or do you like eating out? Are you a home body or do you like to travel the globe? You can have a Ferrari if you want one and God won't be mad at you, but let me just say this; your goal has to line up with your value because you may want the Ferrari. It's shiny, beautiful and valuable to you. You may want that and you go after that, but maybe that doesn't match your life goal. The income you would have to have to get and maintain that is different than the life value that you have designed.
You may have to be on the road or out of town; what's your value? Is it important for you to be able to serve in your church? Be able to give? To be able to love and to serve in the community; is that important to you? If it is, then that design needs to be filtered and your goals need to be filtered through that design. As you design your life goal and you filter your values through what's most important, it will help you design a quality life to live. Your highest goal is love, and to remember your "why." I've talked about the "why" all through this book. Your "why" is your reason. It's the reason when all hell breaks loose against you, when bad things happen to you, your "why" will give you energy to get up another day and to go fight again. When the doctor's report says you don't have much time left or this is a bad situation, when the pink slip comes, when the business fails, when the marriage is struggling, the "why" keeps your head above water. It is the reason why you'll

come back to church next week. It's the reason you'll feed your kids. It's the reason you get up again.

You have to have a strong "why". I've told you this before and I'll tell you again, when my dad passed away, he didn't have a strong "why" to stick around and so he left when the time was right for him. There really, really wasn't a reason for him to be here. He had no "why" left. Yes, he left earlier than he had to have, but you know what? Like Job says in Job 6:11, *"what strength do I have left that I can go on hoping? What goal do I have that I would prolong my life?"* One version said, *"what goal do I have that would motivate me to fight to stay?"* Maybe it's your children; maybe it's what you want to do for the kingdom of God. I encourage you to have a "why." I tried to talk my dad into a "why" and every time I'd bring something up, he'd go *"eh, heaven's looking real good to me."* And you know what? That's okay. Paul said the same thing. Paul said *"Hey, I'm going to stick around for a while because of the why of you, but he's like, heaven, I could go today."* When somebody threatened to kill Paul he'd go, would you? Would you please? For most of us we'd be crying and begging the person not to kill us. Then we have Paul begging for death.

Write and Review (Dream A Little Dream With Me)

Number two, you've got to write it down and you've got to review it often. The weakest ink is stronger than the strongest mind because there's something about writing it down and visiting it. The cool thing is that you can dream about it and you can throw that piece of paper away, you can throw that book away and write a new one if you want. It can change, but get it on paper.

Ephesians 3:20 God can do more than you've ever dreamed of.

I love that verse! But what I've discovered is that a lot of us, because our dreams and our imagination are so big, live with disappointment because we go on without doing the little stuff. You may not be able to have the big stuff right away and then become disappointed, thinking that God doesn't love you as much as somebody else. Here's how you do it. You need to have the big dreams; you need to suspend yourself in reality for a minute. If money was no object, if time was no issue, what would you do, where would you go? What kind of a life would you have? Use your imagination and then you need to get some of those dreams on paper. But then, come back down out of the clouds, this is where a lot of us don't do that, we just keep the big dreams in our head, write those things down, they may change, they may ebb and flow, the things you wanted ten years ago, you might not want today, but things will change. Come back down out of the clouds and figure out what you want to have happen this year. What do I want to have happen over the next six months? What do I want over the next ninety days? What do I want to have happen next week? And then write down some obtainable, measurable goals that you can live out over the next twenty four hours, over the next week, over the next two weeks, over the next three months.

There is something that you have to have for you to be an overcomer; it's called the big MO. It's called momentum and if all you have are the big dreams and the big wishes, that's all they really are; wishes without a plan. You have to have some accomplishments that are giving you fuel to look forward. Tomorrow's going to be a great day because today was a great day. If you really want to get the momentum flowing and get the momentum going in your direction, then you and I need to have some victory goals that happen just on a daily basis, on a weekly basis, on a three month basis, what could you do? Make five more phone calls? Absolutely! Apply for a job, apply for that college, send out a resume, invite someone over, ask the girl out on a date? What if she says no? Well, you don't have her right now anyway, ask her out! Are you with me? Now if you're married don't be doing that! That was for single people!

Get down to where you give yourself some victories on a short term basis and achieve those short term victories. Go bid some jobs, go make a loan application for your new business, do something so that you'll be able to say "*I did that, I did these five things, I did that.*" Are you with me? There is no energy like the energy of the big MO when it goes in your flow.

Habakkuk 2:2 The Lord said, write the vision, make it clear on tablets so that anybody that reads it can read it quickly.

It needs to be short, sweet and succinct. The vision will happen at the appointed time, because there is an appointed time. If you have a vision and it's written down, there's an appointment. You've got an appointment coming just like a doctor's appointment… there's a vision appointment. The vision will happen at the appointed time, it hurries towards the goal and it won't be a lie. If it delays, then wait for it, because it certainly will happen and it won't be late. You are an overcomer, you're a winner, and you are a champion because that's who God sees you as. Hang onto the vision and hang onto the dream. Write it down.

Evaluate the Dream

Third, you need to review your dream and evaluate where you are right now. You do this because it helps you realize where you are going. You know that you are not there yet, but you are here. You are not where you used to be and God is good. You have accomplished some good things and God has been faithful to you and when you do that, then you're able to look forward. You realize that your past has been good and that helps you to believe for some more in the future.

God does have great plans for you and he's going to do some incredible things in your lives, in your families and in your church family. The scripture says in Zachariah 4:6, "*You will not succeed on your own.*" On your own strength, or by your own power, the scripture says, but by my spirit says the Lord. It's going to be his power and his strength empowering you to do what you can't do on your own.

Proverbs 16:9 We plan the way we want to go, but then it is God who makes us able.

It is God who gives us the power to actually be able to live this dream out and to do the things that he's called us to do. In addition to writing your dreams down, you need to begin to speak positive about those dreams and about your goals. I think a lot of us have self-sabotaged, accidentally, with our own speech to ourselves. Colossians 4:6 says "*Be gracious in your speech.*" The goal is to bring out the best in others in conversation, when you are talking to another person, you would never put them down or cut them off. However, people often do cut themselves off and put themselves down. It's not just the others that we need to speak the best about. We need to speak the best about ourselves. Don't make your goal *"I want to lose weight this year."* That's vague and that's a mystery. Instead, say it this way: *"As of June 1 I will weigh 185 pounds."* Say it that way.

You may be thinking, Pastor I've failed before. See the thing is not about the thing; it's what you become and who you become in the process of pursuing your goal. It's not about the goal, it's about your discipline, it's about your behavior and it's about your life. It's about you obtaining the life that God has for you. I promise you that if you write this down and you begin to speak in the positive, you will make a change and you will reach your goals. Someone might be saying that they want to have a better marriage. Don't say I want a better marriage; say I will have a better, more intimate marriage. And then you'll find yourself as you begin to confess that and speak that, you'll find yourself doing the things necessary for that to happen. It's in you becoming, not pursuing.

I've discovered also that what we pursue, we often lose. Our goals often times can be like butterflies. Have you ever tried to chase butterflies? They're hard to catch! I mean you've got to get them sitting still because when they are flying you are out of luck. You might catch one accidentally but that is about it. I'm just saying to you, what you and I need to do is become the person that attracts the butterfly. Some of you are looking at me like what's he mean by that? Well, let me give you an example. When I first started liking my wife, Laura, I was attracted to her, but as I began to pursue her she backed off. She didn't want to be smothered. So I stopped and I thought about what kind of a guy would she be attracted to, that she would pursue? And then I tried to write those things down and I tried to become that guy. It must have worked because we've been married now for twenty three years, but I've been with her for twenty five years, so it must have worked because she stayed. I didn't run her off right? And often times it is the pursuit of our goal that pushes it further away, but when we become the people that attract success, that attract the relationship, that attract the healthy marriage, we also attract our goals.

Remember to manage your mouth. Someone said to me after one of the services, *"Oh Pastor I heard your message, but oh that's hard!"* Don't say it's hard; instead say *"Oh, that's new!"* You know, I mean at least that's not negative. It is new and maybe you've never talked this way before, but don't make it harder on yourself by saying that it is going to be hard. You just made it hard because you said it's going to be hard. Instead say this is new! That's a good thing, you can move into new things. So have these short term goals, say it in the now.

Chapter 7
Be Inducted Into the Faith Hall of Fame

"The first principle of contract negotiations is don't remind them of what you did in the past - tell them what you're going to do in the future." – Stan Musial

Faith is; perceiving as real fact when it is not revealed to the senses. What I see, taste, touch, smell and hear! I only have five senses but maybe God has fifteen senses available and he only gave humanity five of them, I don't know. I do know that scientists tell us, and I believe this is true, that the physical realm that we live in gives us the ability to only know of three or four dimensions. Those scientists tell us that there are quite possibly eleven dimensions if not more. God is God, I'm not and I'm going to tell him how everything's going to be. He's God, I'm not God; and so I need to have faith. What is faith? Faith is the connector between my senses; what I see, taste, touch, smell and hear. Faith is the connector between that and the eleven dimensions or more of spirit realm; of the thing that I don't have yet. When I have faith it's the title deed. It's the sign off and the assurance that what I'm believing for, when it's filtered through the values and a God-first life, is on the way. Even though I don't have it yet, that I do have it. I've got the title to it but it just hasn't been delivered it yet. But it's on the way!

That's what a goal is.

Hebrews 11:1 Now faith is the assurance, it's the confirmation, the title deed of watch, the things we hope for, being the proof of the things we don't see and the conviction of their reality.

And so these little short term goals, these little victories, they give us that momentum to stay in the game. They give us the momentum to hang in there and when all hell's breaking loose, you are accomplishing the little things that give you the victories. Now it is time for you to abandon those limiting beliefs that every one of us have. There's a thermostat on the wall, that thermostat is set at a set point, it's set for comfort. Now we all have different opinions of what comfort is. Some are cold, some are wrapped up and some are

burning up, so we all have that different set point. Your soul has a set point of comfort for you and what many of us do at this point is say *"I'm not worthy of this."* You are always disappointed, even though you don't want to be disappointed. Even though you don't want bad stuff to happen to you, you are always the victim.
The set point of your soul says, *"I'm the victim, I'm the loser, I'm this, I'm that"*, that's why psychologists have studied those people we talked about before who have won the lottery and then within five to ten years they don't have any money left! How could it be? Millions of dollars gone! It is because the set point of their soul is telling their brains that things are too uncomfortable, whether you're above or beneath, this is too uncomfortable for them and so they self-sabotage to bring themselves back to their set point.

Reset Your Thermostat

What do we need to do? Renew our mind with the word of God to change the set point of what is normal for us. The best way that I could describe it to you is this: This guy I know had a dog in his yard and his dog always chased other dogs. *"Woof, woof, woof"*, he'd run after the other dogs as the dogs would come by his yard. You've seen those dogs before, you may even have one. And so what he had to do was chain his dog to a big oak tree in the front yard and put a twenty foot chain on it. He said he felt so sorry for the dog because for the first two months the dog would be sitting on the porch and another dog would come running by and that dog would take off, woof, woof, woof and he'd hit the end of that chain and it about yanked his head off. The dog did it time after time and he said he thought that the dog must be stupid!

But then he noticed that after a couple months of this, that the dog didn't do that anymore. That the dog would always take off after the dog, but stop right before the limitations of that chain. One day, this guy was out working in his yard and he unhooked the collar from the chain and he thought that as long as he was out there with him, even though the dog was off of his chain, he would surely not run off. He took the chain off but left the collar on. Then sure enough, he's sitting there and it wasn't that much longer and a dog comes by, *"woof, woof"* he takes off after him. The man thought the dog was going to run out in the street, but sure enough, though the dog was free, the dog stopped at that same spot where the chain had once stopped him. He thought to himself, *you're free and you don't know it.*

God says to you today, you're an overcomer, abandon those limiting beliefs.

YOU'RE FREE AND YOU DON'T KNOW IT!

When you accept Christ and you are born again, all things are made new. The scripture says that you're a new creation in Christ Jesus; all things are made new, altogether new in you. I had a limiting self-belief that I was a shy person. I did! Everybody else would have said the same thing about me, that I was just a shy guy. I thought that because of past behavior, past experiences and even because of the labels that other people gave me, so I was scared. And when I began to feel God saying what he wanted me to do what I'm doing up here today, I had an inner conflict. How many of you know that my thermostat was jacked up? I was uncomfortable. So I stepped into a realm of uncomfortable but I discovered as I got used to it, that the shyness wasn't there anymore and all of a sudden I realized that I can chase the big dog now! *"Woof, woof"* and I don't care what anybody thinks about me anymore! I don't have to be dignified. I don't have to be perfect. And I don't have to have everybody approve or like me.

There are just some people that won't like you. The quicker you come to that reality, the happier you'll be in your life. When your being who God created you to be, there'll be a whole bunch of people that will like you even more. And I want to say to you, abandon those limiting beliefs. Your marriage is this or that. Your finances are always this. That you are disorganized, you're scatterbrained or you are horrible with money. You're a new creation in Christ Jesus and you can be organized. You can be great with money. You can build businesses. You can do great things and God's going to knit you together to help each other to do those things.

The C Word

Finally, here comes the big one, commitment. We live in a commitment phobic society. Because commitment lowers our options; when you commit to something you're saying now, all these other things are no. When I said yes to Laura, my wife, it meant that I couldn't date other people. Are you with me? And so it lowers the options. We live in a society where we value options often times above commitment! But I want you to know something, if you're going to accomplish anything great it's going to take commitment.

Recently I watched a televised funeral of a great baseball player, Stan Musial. As I watched, there were a couple of things about it that were unbelievable. I thought about Stan Musial's life and what he accomplished. Married to the same woman for seventy two years, that's a great accomplishment in today's world isn't it? Awesome! The other thing is he turned down more money. I felt sorry for Albert Pujols sitting there as they were talking about how Stan could have taken more money and he could have went to a bigger market than St. Louis to play baseball. Albert's sitting there frowning. Yes, he had a different vision than Stan, different goals. Anyway, so Stan could have had more money, he could have gone to a bigger market, but he was committed to the consistency of his friends, of his teammates, of his family and to the City of St. Louis. That was where he had decided to commit. I thought about how that kind of guy, a Hall of Famer, a world classer, a champion, never achieves the Hall of Fame in one weekend, in one season, or in one great game. A Hall of Famer becomes a Hall of Famer because of commitment, consistency and the methodical behavior of doing something over and over and over and over and over again.

As Bob Costas did the eulogy for Stan Musial, he said *"You know Hollywood wasn't attracted to Stan Musial because we, human nature, our news media, Hollywood, we like the drama."* Isn't it funny how you're going down the interstate and your traffic backs up, when you get up to the accident, it wasn't even on your side of the road, it was on the other side, but the reason your traffic is slowing down is because everybody is rubber-necking? And when you get up to the accident, what do you do? You slow down and look too! Why? Because we love the drama, we love the blood, the guts and the gore. We love the violence. We love the news reports that are the murders, the robberies, the tragedies and the fires. Those things draw the crowds. Bob Costas said that Hollywood never made a movie about Stan the Man because Stan didn't have any drama. He wasn't having affairs on his wife. He didn't go through four, five or ten divorces. He wasn't addicted to drugs or alcohol. He was too boring for Hollywood!

I thought about that and I thought, you know, that should be the earmark for us. Yeah we all have drama that's happened to us in the past and I get it. We all have the drama... play down the drama, don't let the drama be your story. Let your story be a story of commitment and consistency. Let your story be that you get the base hits, that you get the runs. Develop an automatic system to do this. The way you get the consistency and commitment is to develop great habits and great routines. And that's kind of what the baby dedication is about. A parent is saying, *"I'm going to develop the routine of being in church, raising my children in church, showing up for church, serving in church, getting up and reading my Bible, praying, talking to God. I'm going to work out; I'm going to eat the right foods."* Oh, it's only one doughnut. Yeah, but it's one doughnut every day. Or maybe like me, four doughnuts every day! I don't do that anymore, but there was a time in my life where I did and man, it caught up with me.

What happens to us is we give our self a pass once in a while on the small things, and all of a sudden the thing that you value most, your family and your children are lost. You leave this planet early; you leave the things you valued most, because you craved the simple thing of a doughnut too many times in a row over a consistency of a long period of time. You are overcomers and every person here, every single one, though you may not see it right now, every single one of you are potential Hall of Famers. And I don't mean in sports, I mean in faith.

And man, there's some people listed in the Faith Hall Of Fame, and if you think you don't qualify... there's prostitutes in there, there's murderers in there... you're qualified. In fact, murderers wrote most of the scripture; Moses murdered, David murdered, I mean these guys were some bad dudes. You're not disqualified. You're a Hall of Famer, you're a victor, you're a conqueror, you're a winner, you're a champion and though you may not be where you want to be yet, you're not going to get there in a weekend. You're not going to get there overnight. This is a lifetime and you've got to realize you've only got today. So get up to bat and swing to hit the ball today. Steal a base today, run today, put on the uniform, put the jersey on, volunteer, get involved and serve God! You only have today. The way to have a great life is to start today.

Get some small victories under your belt and get that big MO going in your favor. MO is momentum. In fact, that's the title of the next chapter: Stop the Drama and Get the Big MO in your Favor. Maybe you're reading this today and you maybe believe in God, but maybe you don't have that born again experience where I talked about all things being made new on the inside of you? Maybe someone gave you this book and you are thinking to yourself, "*I want to make Him not only my Savior, but also my Lord.*" Lord is a word that in our language would be a manager, boss, chief or ruler. You may be thinking, "*I want to make sure that I'm accepted, Jesus Christ, that I'm born again, that I've got that thing going on where I'm made new.*" God not only gives you a fresh start with your sins being forgiven, cleansed, washed away, sorrow being removed, guilt being removed, but he also imparts in you spiritual attributes and spiritual gifts that you may not even realize that are available to you. I didn't know I could be a pastor. But when I was born again, all of a sudden he began to call me into this. Maybe you have done that before but you want to make a new commitment to God. Maybe you need to let go, abandon. This simple prayer is a great way to end this chapter.

Father, I receive your forgiveness. I ask you to come into my heart. I thank you that my shame, that my guilt, my past has been forgiven and that we have eternal life in you. I thank you for a fresh start and a new beginning. Now Father I ask you to fill me with your Holy Spirit today and may I experience newness of life, new beginnings and fresh starts, and may you also give me gifts, talents and abilities that I didn't even know were capable coming out of me. In Jesus' name we pray. Amen! I'm excited for you! That's good stuff!

Chapter 8
Less Drama, More Momentum

"Change hurts. It makes people insecure, confused, and angry. People want things to be the same as they've always been, because that makes life easier. But, if you're a leader, you can't let your people hang on to the past." –Richard Marcinko, Seal Team Six

In this chapter you are going to learn how to have a great bounce back response. You will never make it to the Hall of Fame in a season. You will never make it to the Hall of Fame of life or the Hall of Fame of faith or anything really great, unless you have the ability to get back up once life knocks you down. Because the truth is that life is tough, it is hard in this world, and Jesus said, *"You will have trouble, be of good cheer though because I've overcome the world for you on your behalf for you."* But you and I still have to fight this battle in our mind. It's called the battle of faith and we're going to talk about faith.

Yes, we've talked about faith through this series. Faith is in every installment because in order for us to receive the dream, the goal, the hope, the thing that's out there before us, in order for you to do that, we have to have faith. Faith means that you have something you don't have in the natural yet, but in the spirit you're receiving it. You are receiving it in the spirit because it's out there and it's yours. You can have it, but you don't have it in the five senses yet; what you see, taste, touch, smell and hear. You're not experiencing the "it" yet. Learn to use that word yet. It's coming and it's on the way.

Have you discovered in life there's always drama all around? Have you ever seen those people that can take a little bit of drama and turn it into huge drama? We all know somebody out there that can turn a molehill into a mountain, per the cliché. Those people (maybe it's you) can take something that's "not a big deal" and make it a big, huge, gigantic, overwhelming deal. I want to teach you how to have less drama and more momentum. The reason I use momentum is because if you're going to have a great bounce back response in becoming that person that God says that you can become, you and I have to learn how to have a great bounce back. Boom!

Do you remember the little rock'em, sock'em toys? I use to love them when I was a kid. The harder you hit them, the quicker they come back up. And that's YOU! We've got a great bounce back response, that's who we are. Now, to go into this, there's a foundational scripture.

Galatians 6:9 Let us not become weary in doing well for at the proper time we will reap a harvest if you don't quit.

If, the big if… circle the word up there if you're a note taker and if you're not a note taker circle the word if; IF you don't quit, if you don't give up. The key is to not quit. You could stop reading this right now. Just quit. Give up. I am your cheerleader and I'm cheering you on not to quit. Stay in the game okay? I want to help you and before I get to the how to, how to have a great bounce back; I want you to understand the process of faith. You need to understand how the process works. It works the same for you as it did for Abraham, Noah, Nehemiah, Jesus, King David, all of the heroes of the faith… it works the same. The same process they went through is the same process you and I have to go through in the process of our faith development. That dream, that goal, that word from God; it's the same process.

Decide To Dream

The first part of the process is when God gives you a dream, God gives you hope. Maybe you're sitting in a church service and God begins to speak a dream to you. Maybe you're watching an infomercial. Did you know God can speak to you in an infomercial? And maybe you're at a Cardinal baseball game or a football game or a hockey game. God speaks to me in all those environments. Maybe you are at a movie theater or you are lying in your bed. God can speak to you anywhere, but what happens is God encounters our life, we have an experience with God and we get a dream, we get a hope, we get a vision of what could be and what might be.

We can see visions of a better marriage, of a better job, a business, starting a business, getting free from this, starting this or that and we get this hope and we get this dream. You can go back through the

Bible and look at Noah. God spoke to Noah and gave him a dream to build this ark, so Noah worked on this thing for over one hundred years. All of the people made fun of him, not a drop of rain for a hundred years and he's working on an ark. I mean that really takes faith guys, come on. What God asks of you is so minimal in comparison to what he asked of our ancestors.

You look at that, then you look at Abraham, God has a word for Abraham, you're going to be the father of many nations but first you must sacrifice your son. WHAT? Can you imagine God asking you to do that today? Then there was Joseph. God visits Joseph and said you're going to rule over your people, your own brothers; you're going to rule over them. Big mistake telling his brothers that dream; a lot of problems came after that. But the dream did manifest. Moses, Moses had a dream, a word from God, that he would lead his people free from captivity, out of bondage. I mean you go on through scripture and the dreams, the visions, the impossibilities are all there. Nehemiah had a dream, David had a dream.
The funny thing about David is that the prophet came to David and anointed him King, spoke a word over him telling him that he's going to be the new king of Israel and it's going to be this awesome thing. See, what first happens is that even Jesus had a dream that he would set the world free from sin. God speaks to your inward heart and in your mind. You receive it and then the next thing that has to happen in this process of faith that happens in all of us, it's a common denominator, in order for us to reach this dream and fulfill this vision that God has given us. We have to make a decision.

Dream, Faith, ACTION!

We have to take action. We have to do something so that God speaks a word and then out of that word we have to by faith, do something, sign up for the class, submit a resume, fill out a job application, ask her out on a date, ask him out on a date. Is it okay to do that? Yes, girls can ask guys out on dates. At least it is okay in my world. Maybe your world's different. Anyway, you have to do something, you have to step out and make a decision. You have to invest in the dream. You have to maybe spend some money, spend some time, some research, some study and then after you've invested and done that, you have to let go of some things. Did you know that part of the process of achieving a dream is letting go? You have to let go of your safety and security, the familiar, the comfortable that you've always known. Often times you have to let go of those things, and man, that's often times hard to do because you're so familiar with them. But you have to let go in order for you to move into what God has for you. You've got to let go of the safety and security that we all have been taught all of our lives. That one factor is paramount.

The most incredible thing you can have in your life, what our society has taught us, is safety and security. I love safety and security, but I want you to know something, you will never achieve anything great in your life clinging to safety and security. You always have to take some calculated faith risks. You just do. It is a requirement of doing anything out of the ordinary and anything great. So focus in, act on and let go.

We're fine with faith at this point in the process because we've got the dream and we acted on it. We're excited and at this point we're typically passionate, jazzed, caffeinated and all juiced up. On Fire! Then something happens, and this is the process of faith; I want you to know something, this happens to everybody, delay happens. Now in my world I like to think delay is demonic. I like to think delay is the devil. Delay is no good. I love microwaves, I love the fast lane. I love speed, I love going. I don't like to waste time. I'm hyper. I want it now and I want it right now. That's not just me though, that's our culture. A mistake that a lot of people make is that they think that because they are in a delay and things aren't happening as fast as they want them to happen, that either they did something wrong and maybe that God's upset with them or that maybe they missed the voice of God. Things aren't going so well because we're in a delay and often times we equate delay with a "no" from God.

As if God's saying no to us just because it's not happening on our time table. I've got good news for you here…I've got good news for you.

The good news is that you're right on schedule! The process and the timing of it is right on track. So don't be discouraged because the enemy wants to take the delay, the waiting, and turn it into a problem. Life is full of delays. We cling to the safety and the security of our past. Is the only way that you can really, truly be safe and secure to be six feet under and horizontal? Then you're safe and you're secure and it's all good. But until then, you're living life, you're going to have some risks and opposition, you're going to have some delays. It's part of the process. When this happens remember that it is part of the process of life. Delays and waiting is all part of it. Savor the delay. At the hospital they have a waiting room. At the doctor's office they have a waiting room. What do you do when you get stuck in traffic? You wait. What do you do at the airport? You get there early and you wait in line and then once you get through the line you wait for your plane and then the plane is late and you wait some more. You wait, you wait. Tom Petty says the waiting's the hardest part! And it is, isn't it? Don't you detest waiting?

It's just horrible, the waiting part, I don't like it, but it is part of the process and you're in good company when you have to wait.

Everyone, I mean you could go through that same list of guys that I just mentioned, had to wait. Moses, think about Moses. He got a word from God that he would lead his people out of captivity and he probably had in his mind that he was going to bring them out of Egypt into the promised land next week or if not next week for sure the week after, but you all know the story. Forty years later he's not even in the Promised Land yet. I mean look at King David, David gets a word from God, he's anointed by God, he has a dream, he has hope, anointed, and what does he do? He spends the next several years of his life running from people trying to slay him and kill him, living in caves and holes. A King? Hey, God I think maybe you missed something here, what's up? I'm living in a cave, you, through your spokesmen, I mean I didn't say it, your spokesmen said it, I'm a king and you got me. You got the King, Lord, you've got the king in a cave. The king is in a cave.

Let me be your spokesmen for just a second because if you're like me in any way shape or form, the delay is a bummer and sometimes I want to scream, *"Hey God, you're the one that gave me the dream, I mean if you're not going to bring the dream about then why did you give it to me? God?"* So let me be your spokesmen, God, what are you waiting on for these people of yours? Right? Do you ever feel that way? You're in good company though, because these guys went through the same thing. Noah spent a whole hundred years building an ark. It hadn't rained, now think about this; he gets on the zoo (ark) and he has to put snakes by birds. You don't put snakes and birds together in one place like that. Can you imagine what that was like? See the practical aspect of it? By the way, when I get to heaven, I want to ask him why didn't he just go ahead and kill those last two mosquitos.

The process of faith is that you get the dream from God, you take action, you step out and then God says wait. And we, in our instant gratification culture, go no God we don't want to wait. And then difficulties come. Struggle and hardships come and we begin to really question God and doubt ourselves. Maybe we think God changed his mind. Typically at this point we hit a phase of a dead end, like the children of Israel when they heard the word from the Lord they were delivered and then what happens to them? They come up against the Red Sea. Many of them began to murmur think that it was better back in Egypt; at least they had a place to lay their head. Here they were going to be eaten up by their enemies.
And the dead end aspect; think about Abraham. Abraham got a word from God that he was going to be the father of many nations and things just weren't happening. He took matters into his own hands when he decided that God was taking too long. So they had an Ishmael, a flesh, a baby out of the flesh. It wasn't the promise of God, but because the delay was so long and because the difficulty was so long, he quit waiting for God and instead took things into his own hands. So all of a sudden now he's up to ninety nine years old.

Now do the math on the logic of this. You heard a word from God and you have to be thinking that God must have really messed up. Everything quit working. He was as good as dead. There was no little blue pill, there wasn't that, no everything was as good as dead, it didn't work anymore. Let me tell you something, God is the God of the resurrection! That little boy in Sunday school had it right, he had it right. God is that God.

You may feel like you're at a dead end in your life and that everything has stopped. You may think that the doors are closed and that there's no way out. Jesus and his own disciples had a dream.

Jesus had told them that he's a king and yet the king dies on the cross. He's in the ground. God's specialty is taking defeated situations and turning them in to miracles. It's all part of the process of your faith. If you're in the dead end situation, in the discouragement, in the difficulty, in the delay; let me say something, you're right on track with all of these guys, these heroes of the faith. You're in good company so don't quit now. Please don't quit because the only way you really lose is if you quit. But if you hang in there and you don't quit, you're going to come out of this thing for sure. You will be a hero.

Train Like A Navy Seal

Let go of your tendency to always want to be right about everything.

Don't point fingers again! You know that person that just can't be wrong because their insecurity is so forefront that they have to be right about everything? If you really want to go forward, if you really want to advance in life; let go of your tendency to always want to be right. Breathe deep with me. I don't have to be right about everything and it's totally okay. Breathe deep again, okay, it's okay.

Next, learn to be flexible and to bend without breaking. Let life deal you some blows and you give and you flow. I love judo because judo is the movement with the flow of the body, not resistance against. Let go of your need to always want to have to be right and learn to be flexible, bendable and learn to go with the flow of what God is doing. If it means wait, then wait; because the breakthrough's coming. Don't quit! Keep depending on God that your breakthrough is on its way. It's part of the process, it might be five years, it might be ten years, it might be twenty years, but don't quit.

2 Corinthians 1:8 We don't want you to be in the dark friends about how hard it was when all of this came down on us in Asia Provence, it was so bad we ourselves didn't even think we were going to make it. We felt like we had been sentenced to death row and that it was over for us. As it turns out it was the best thing that could have ever happened. Instead of trusting in our own strength or wit to get us out of it, we were forced to trust God totally.

Not a bad idea since he's the one who raises the dead and he did it. He rescued you from certain doom and he'll do it again, rescuing you as many times as you need rescued. And I just want to say to you, whatever you're going through, even if it seems hard and like you've been sentenced to death row, it's not tomorrow yet. Your marriage is over, you've got a deed and no job, the business and the career and everything's dead; listen, it's not tomorrow yet. Those of you that have walked with God for just a little bit, you know this, you have this testimony that you were at a bad place maybe five or ten years ago and it was horrible. You thought you were done for but somehow here you are five or ten years later and you could teach and preach to each one of us how you made it through that hard time. You don't know how you got through, but here you are today. You're still breathing. You can still smile. You're here today. It ain't over! The divorce didn't kill you. The bankruptcy didn't kill you. The hard times didn't kill you. You're still here.

That's the way it is with God. You're in the process. What you're going through is part of the process because it's not the goal that's the big epitome of life, it's not the obtaining of the goal; it's who you become as you move toward the goal. It's what God makes out of you and who you are and how you develop through that and what you accomplish along the journey. There's something about that, even if you're in a prison and I don't mean a literal prison, I'm talking about the prison of bondage; of an addiction or a marriage.

Did you know that a job, a certain job could feel like prison to you? You don't feel like you have options and this job is draining the life out of you. You feel imprisoned in this situation, listen, I have encouraging news for you today. You're in the process so don't give up, they key is to not give up.

So, how do you have a great bounce back response when you had a dream that filled you with passion; you were just jazzed, juiced and excited about it, all pumped up about it, but today you've had the wind knocked out of you. The drama has stolen your momentum and you don't feel the juice anymore? You're simply going through the motions, so what do you do? I'm going to take you through some training. You ready to go through some Navy Seal training?

This guy I know was a memory champion. He wasn't that way in college. In college he had a 1.25 grade point average and they were going to kick him out. Anyway, he began to study memory and how to increase and improve his memory. He began to get so good at his memory that he competed in a national competition. Two years in a row he came in fourth place and he decided to do something different because he didn't feel like he was able to break that barrier, to beat these other four people that were winning the championships, and so he hired a Navy Seal.

This was a very famous Navy Seal, he wasn't a memory champion guy, but this guy was great at training people and coaching people and so he hired him. He asked the young man how all of the other competitors in this memory contest were training. And the guy said that they go into a quiet room, a private room, a bedroom or an office. They close the door and zone out all distractions. They get in the quiet and try to get in the zone; then they practice and practice and practice.

The Navy Seal told him that they were going to do exactly the opposite. They were going to go to the public swimming pool where all of the kids are swimming and playing and splashing to train. Not only were they going to this loud place, but they were not going to train on top of the water, but on the bottom of the pool and for as many seconds as his breath could be held. They were going to train under water. So he told them that he will train for 20-30 seconds and pop up for a breath of air and then go back down. And he did this, and he did this for several weeks. Well one day he wakes up feeling horrible, he had the flu and he says that he had a 102 temperature, and he did what most of us would do, he began to feel sorry for himself.

So he called his Navy Seal buddy to tell him that he couldn't train because he was sick. The trainer responded with, "*AWESOME! We couldn't have asked for a better situation than this! This is awesome! Look, I know you're feeling horrible, but if you've ever trained any day you've got to train today. Because you will have such an advantage over your competitors, I promise you none of them are going to train sick and none of them are going to train in the bottom of a pool sick. What if on the day of the competition you've got a 102 fever? This will be easy "schmeezy" for you because you've trained with a 102 fever under water!"*

So he did it. He trained, underwater, with a 102 degree fever and it was miserable. The Navy Seal told him that the seals make their training much harder than actual combat so that when they are in combat, they can look back on training and feel like the situation that they are currently in is easy. This is real world stuff; the hard stuff was in training. Sure enough on the day of the competition, he wasn't sick, but he had only gotten one hour of sleep the night before. For the next two years in a row Ron White took first place and the championship. He became number one and so can you.

Chapter 9
Get Down With LTP (Yeah You Are Free)

Optimism is the faith that leads to achievement. Nothing can be done without hope and confidence. - Helen Keller

You can start your training by identifying yourself as an "LTP". Long Term Player! You can't become a world class, Hall of Famer in one season or two. You have to decide to go for the career. If you're going to be world class, and you are world class, then you have to decide, I'm an LTP. And if you really want to have fun with it, look into a mirror and tell yourself that you are an LTP. You're a long term player. You're not testing this religion thing out and seeing if it works, you're not here for just a little while. Tell yourself, *"I'm in, I'm all in and I'm all in for eternity."*

So you're a long term player. If you're going to get this faith process, you've got to make your mind up that you are in this for the long haul. Have some fun with it. Rap it. Sing it. Write it down. Make it fun. You're an LTP, a Long Term Player and you're in this thing to win, not quit. Ephesians says that *"because God will help you out, you're going to withstand, you're going to endure, you're going to make it."* Ephesians is my favorite book in the Bible. In it,

Paul gives the church instruction on how to overcome.

When there is a football game, they're going to have helmets on, right? The team pays for those players to have helmets; they don't even have to pay for their own helmet. God gives you your suit-up equipment to go out on the field and play the game of life. So here's what he says in verse 11, *"Put on God's whole armor which God supplies, that you may be able to successfully stand up against all the strategies and deceits of the devil. Resist and stand your ground on the day of danger. And having done all that the crisis demands stand firmly in your place. Take up the shield of faith which you can extinguish all the flaming arrows of the evil one. Be strong, be courageous, stay in the game, don't quit."*

Sometimes it just means that you dig in and just don't quit. That you're there and you've made up your mind that you're a long term player and you're here to stay. You're not going anywhere, you're in the game. This is the key; this is paramount, this is foundational because if you have any quit in you, any option to quit, the enemy will push, push, push, push and push to take you to that point. You just have to make him think you're messed up because the enemy has no wisdom. When he sees you going through all the stuff that you go through and you still come to church and lift your hand, sing the songs and smile. You still greet, still usher, still run cameras and still live life; the enemy has to scratch his head because he doesn't understand.

He has to scratch his head because it doesn't make sense to him. He has no wisdom.

Focus On Hope

You're a winner and you're a champion. You're not a quitter so go for it. Because a long term player has got to have a vision. Next you have to focus on the solution, not the problem; that's the hardest one for a lot of us because the problem screams our name. *"Come here and look at me!"* You know the squeaky wheel? It always makes all the noise doesn't it? And your problems are like that squeaky wheel. Your problems are always screaming, hollering out *"Hey give me the attention! Tim, Lisa, look over here!"* Your problem is always begging you to give it attention, but instead you will look at the solution. Keep your eyes on the solution, not the problem, not the situation, not the circumstance, but the hope.

In World War Two there was a Navy cruiser that was carrying one thousand and one hundred people on the ship. The ship was shot by Japanese torpedoes and as that ship began to sink the men bailed into the water. They were frigid waters. Over the next five days two-thirds of the shipmates died and passed away because of hunger, hypothermia, drowning and shark attacks; a lot of the men died. The waters began to separate many of them leaving ten men together with one young officer among them. The young officer began to do something to keep the hope alive in these guys; he began to focus not on the problem, not on the situation, but on the solution. He started to ask them about their families. What did their wives look like? How old were their children? He'd say *"Bill tell me about your wife, what does she look like? Do you have children? Describe your children, how old are they?"* He began to get them to go into great detail with questions like, *"Are her lips thin or are they thick? Big ears, little ears, big nose, little nose, what she look like? What do the kids look like? What are their names? Tell me their names, tell me their ages? Ed, what do you think they're going through right now? No doubt they've heard that our ship was sunk. You think they're fearful right? Isn't it awful that that they're feeling that way?"*

He told them to think with him. What an ingenuous young man he was, telling these men to imagine vividly the things that they had to go home to. The things that they needed to survive for. He went so far as to have them describe back to him what it was going to be like when they see their families again for the first time. He asked for all of the details. *"What are you going to do? What's going to be happening? What are the tears looking like? Are they little bitty tears, are they just puddles? Or are they big crocodile tears running down the face? What will you do? Will you pick the kid up? Will you hug the kid?"* He began to focus on what could be and what's going to be.

History records that none of those men that kept those hopes alive perished, not one.

What was it that caused them against all odds and against natural hope to hang in there another minute, another hour, another month, another day? It was the fact that they kept alive an image of what they were hoping for. You may be going through all kinds of hard times. You may be dealing with some difficulty right now. You may feel like you're at a delay, a dead end, but listen, you're a long term player, an LTP, that's who you are. Not only are you an LTP, but you're focusing on the solution, not the problem. This is the key because it's so easy to focus on the problems.

Helen Keller was once asked if being blind was one of the greatest tragedies in life? She said no, that there's something worse than that. It is that you would have your eyesight and yet not be able to see. And it shocked everyone around and it caused them to wonder what it means to have your eyesight and yet not see. What she was talking about is the ability to see, but not see. I want to challenge you keep your faith alive. Part of being an overcomer is that when things aren't all juiced and jazzy, that you have the ability to have a great bounce back response. That though it's been a tough month, a tough week, a tough year or a tough decade, you have to commit to the idea that you're not quitting, that you're not going anywhere; that you will hang in there.

Put On Some Headphones

Ignore the voices! Let me explain to you what happened in the book of Luke. Jesus was in in the last year, the last week of his life. He was thirty three years old and he was in the last week of his life. By this time there were great crowds all around. Jesus is on his way to Jericho and this blind man was at the gate unable to see anything. As Jesus approached, the blind man was sitting by the roadside begging and when he heard the great crowd going by he asked someone, *"Hey what's happening?"* They told him that Jesus of Nazareth was passing by. He had heard of Jesus before and without hesitation he calls out his name saying, *"Son of David! Have mercy on me!"*

Well this infuriated all the people around him and got them upset. They wondered who this man thought he was to ask for his favor. But Jesus did favor him.

Who do you think that you are to start a business? Why would God want to favor you? Ignore the negative voices around you. Sometimes the most negative voice is not from the ones around me; it's the one inside of my own head. But I've discovered that when you decide to step out in faith, to do something that nobody else is doing, many times it's those closest to you that either attack your dream or they attack you. They want the safety and the security of the familiar. They don't like the change. They want what's comfortable to them and often times you challenge them, even on a subconscious level that they're not moving where they should go. And so those voices often times will become negative and critical. If you're ever going to accomplish anything in your life you have to go through this process of having to ignore the negativity of the voices around us that say you can't do it, and sometimes that voice comes from our own head. Every person of greatness has had to go through this process.

Others challenge us and say, who do you think you are to go for this? You can't do this; you don't have the skill set, the talent or the anointing! Who do you think you are? What do you think you're doing? God's mad at you! Many times you have to learn to ignore the voices. Put on some headphones and play your favorite song as loud as you can and set sail for where you're going.

This young blind man shouted all the more, *"Son of David, have mercy on me!"*

Many times we're living for the approval of parents, bosses, co-workers, children or siblings. You know…the people in our lives and we want their approval. The scripture says that God protects you from all of that. What disapproval in your life do you fear the most? Whose disapproval do you fear the most because the Bible has a word for that: **I-d-o-l,** idol; it's where you put something before God and we inadvertently, often times, put certain people or over what God says.

Proverbs 29:25 The fear of human opinion disables you.

Tell God Your Dreams

Tell God what you want. Always take it to him in prayer. In Luke 18:40 when Jesus came near the blind man at the side of the road, Jesus asked the young man what he wanted him to do for him.

He said, *"Lord, I want to see!"*

It's often the simplest things that we forget to do. The things we need to do to become great are simple and easy to do. The bad news is they're easy not to do. It's easy to tell God what you want but it's also easy to not tell him. I want to encourage you, talk to God and tell God what you want in your life. I want to encourage you when you do tell him, expect him to answer. He's a God that does answer and he will.

Psalms 5:3 In the morning I tell the Lord, in the morning I present my case to the Lord and then I wait expectantly.

Get Off The Couch

The last thing in this process of faith and how to have a great bounce back response is that you've got to come to the place where you take action. You've got to get off the couch, you've got to get out of the bed and you've got to move. Momentum is your friend. What does it take? There's a hunger, there's an appetite for momentum. What will cause us to get momentum in our life and have less drama? You know what it is? It's activity, because sometimes it's as simple as doing an activity. Maybe you just need to clean the closet out, clean the car out, clean something out, organize something, fill out an application, go buy a book, read a book and what creates momentum is a series of little steps. You start running with a step. You run a marathon one step at a time. You run a sprint one step at a time and I just want to tell you that the way to start momentum is to take action.

If you want a better marriage then go buy a book about it, go to a seminar or speak with a counselor. James 2:17 says, "*In the same way faith by itself, if it doesn't accompany action it's dead.*" So you can tell me you have faith out of your mouth, but I'm really watching what you do. Because it's not just what you say, because what you say is important, but it's also what you say accompanied by the activity that you do. So to get the MO going, the big MO, it doesn't have to start big, it just starts with a step.

You already know that I love science and science says that if an object that is sitting still, then it tends to stay sitting still, but if you get the movement going, it tends to move. That's a summary of it, but that's the way life is and the way the Bible is. That's the way your life is. You just have to get the ball rolling. So Jesus is standing there, with this beggar, this blind man beggar asking him to favor him. The crowds are watching and he heals him. He didn't ask him about his past. He didn't ask him about anything. He favored him.

"Receive your sight, your faith has healed you."

And the bible says that immediately he received his sight. What I want to say to you is that those points of breakthrough, though it seems like they've been delayed and there is discouragement, your breakthrough typically comes immediately and you look back and you only remember the breakthrough.

It's going to happen so take action. If you need to receive Christ, receive Christ. If you need to begin to tithe because you need some financial breakthrough, then do it. You know what God's saying to you? He's saying take some action. You need a financial breakthrough? You better start tithing because that's how you get the breakthrough. You take the action. You have a desire for a better marriage, a better plan?

Then take some action! Sign up, make a plan, set some goals, write it down, ink it don't think it. Ink it. Take action!

Pour your spirit out on me today, touch my heart Father and may I realize that you're Lord and though I've hit a dead end, this is the best thing that could have ever happened to me because it causes me to realize that I can't count on myself or my own strength and will or wit, I have to trust in you my Lord, my Savior, my God and I do trust you Lord. I thank you for breakthrough in every area, marital breakthrough, financial breakthrough, addiction breakthrough, relationship breakthrough, break the bondage of depression and discouragement, give hope, fill my heart with joy. Let me begin to enjoy and experience life like never before. In Jesus' name amen!

Chapter 10
Hands Free Zone

"A real decision is measured by the fact that you've taken a new action. If there's no action, you haven't truly decided." -Tony Robbins

This chapter is called Hands Free Zone. What I mean by that zone, specifically, is the self-talk that we all have. If you're going to be an overcomer, and you are, you're an overcomer; if you're going to fulfill your destiny as an overcomer, you have to learn to have great self-talk. We all talk to ourselves on a subconscious level. It's the things you say *about* yourself *to* yourself that can be the problem. Even worse, it's usually not even conscious. If you find yourself saying things like *"this always happens to me,"* then that is not good self-talk.

I'm going to give you a few pointers and try to teach you how to develop a great self-talk. Let's plant the seed on how to start the process of changing the way that you talk to yourself. The phrase *"I need"* is one of the most common and worse phrases that you can have in your vocabulary. *"I need to."* That is future tense and the problem with that is the fact that you never actually get around to *"needing to."* You need to, yeah we all need to. You have to learn to say *"I do, I am, I will, I'm going to now."*

Ephesians 4:29 Do not let any unwholesome talk come out of your mouths, but only what is helpful for building others up according to their need that it may benefit those who listen.

I want to use that scripture for you when you are talking to yourself or about yourself, because somebody's listening to their internal talk. It's you. Let me tell you that the devil, the enemy, he is not your worst enemy. Your worst enemy is sitting in your own seat. The worst enemy is me; I am my own worst enemy. And it is that way with all of us. We sabotage our lives more than the devil sabotages us. Let me give you four things that influence your identity, the way that you see yourself, it is basically your worldview of yourself and how you see yourself.

Number one is your chemistry. Your chemistry is your DNA, the way that you are wired. Some of us have big noses or big ears. Others have a thyroid problem or we have weird toes. Some people have eye issues like not being able to see as well as other people, right? Come on; are we all in the same boat? See, the thing is this: Nobody's perfect and nobody's got it all together. You may be real pretty and real good looking, but you're deficient somewhere else. Because we all are; we're human beings right? So if you're lacking thyroid, go get some thyroid supplements from your doctor. You go see your doctor and they help you to control that issue. So what I'm saying to you is that things depend on how your body's wired, you know your flesh, your propensity towards what you have going on.

Researchers have said that they believe that certain people have a predisposition towards addiction or alcoholism and that some of that is DNA. You know we're all born into sin. Some of us just have certain sins that we have to overcome. You know like doughnut addictions and Dorito's addictions. Others will go a different direction, but we're all born into sin. We've all got it going on so don't ever point fingers at anybody because you've got three of them at least pointing back right at yourself, right?

The second thing is all about your connections. It is about who you are in a relationship with. I could do a whole book on this one! Who you connect with is so important. Show me your friendships and I'll show you your future. Show me your top five friends and I'll show you the mathematic equation of what your life is going to look like in five to ten years. You can't deny it, you can't hide from it. It is the truth of life. Your friendships determine your future.

The third is circumstance. Circumstances are some of the things that shape our self-image, the things that happen to you or around you. You get laid off, a coach yells at you or a parent says some very harsh, cruel, hurtful things to you. You need to learn to embrace the things that happen in your life. Instead of run from them, or even deny them. Some of these things that have happened to you were not good and have possibly even helped shape your identity in a negative way. Your conscience is what you say to yourself about yourself. Things like *"Oh your stupid, what'd you do that for?"*

You may try to make yourself pay for your sin for weeks after you have committed it. I understand repentance and a contrite heart, but not when you let it affect your daily life. Because God doesn't want his children walking around in shame and in defeat, defeated and all beat up. He doesn't want that for you. And so we're not going to live that way, we're going to choose be free.

The fourth and final point is you need to be excited about your choices. Your choices and my choices, they shape our identity. Now here's the cool thing: how many of you have played cards before? There's a wild card in some games. A wild card is a good card, because a wild card can be what you need it to be. Your choices are the wild card of the hand you were dealt in life. A lot of people might say *"Well I was just dealt a horrible hand, I had this big ol' head or this big ol' rear end and I've got this problem or that problem and I was dealt that."* Here's the good news for you: You've also been dealt a wild card! It's called your choices. By your choices you can correct the destiny of your life and go in a direction that will bless you and set you up for great harvest. You get to choose. Choose YOU this day, choose life. Don't you love that? Man, I love that.

Those kinds of things shape us. When I choose the wild card of my sin nature, watch what it does to me… it produces in me feelings of self-condemnation and I condemn myself, I beat myself up. When I choose the wild card and I choose wrong, I choose to go down the path of least resistance and I take the easy way out and I trip up on my sin nature, I feel condemned.

Romans 7:18 I know that I'm rotten inside as far as my old sinful nature is concerned.

And when you choose that wild card, don't you just feel rotten? It's a horrible feeling when you have cooperated with that old enemy of your soul and you choose the wrong things. You just feel horrible, you feel rotten.

I read recently a survey that was conducted among theologians. Over one hundred of them were asked if they were stranded on an island and they could only pick one chapter out of the whole Bible, what chapter would be chosen? Ninety percent of them picked Romans Chapter 8 as their one chapter. The reason why is because Romans Chapter 8 teaches us how to live our lives victoriously as overcomers; are you with me? Now in Romans Chapter 7, Paul sets the stage for us, who we are, as pre-Jesus people, as pre-Christians and as people that are in the process of having their heart renewed. That's where he makes the comment about being rotten inside as far as his old sinful nature is concerned.

When I choose the wild card of my sinful nature, I feel feelings of frustration and I become overwhelmed. Isn't being overwhelmed one of the most obnoxious things? Anybody ever felt overwhelmed before? Feeling overwhelmed is a horrible feeling. As a pastor, if I could help bring healing to people, one of the greatest things that I'd like to bring healing to would be the feeling of being overwhelmed. That is because so many people that I meet, that I work with, so many people are overwhelmed in life; overwhelmed because they have so many things that they need to do. We all have a whole lot to do, but what shuts us down is when we become overwhelmed. We end up not doing any of them. It's like I'm overwhelmed, I'm going to the couch or the bed. I'm overwhelmed, I can't do that well and I've got too many things to do. What happens often times is when we embrace our sinful nature and when we embrace the path of least resistance, we end up being overwhelmed. At least we experience the feelings and the emotions of being overwhelmed. We're going to talk about how to be free from that.

Romans 7:18 No matter which way I turn I can't make myself do right, I'm overwhelmed. I want to, but I can't. When I want to do good, I don't and when I try not to do wrong, I do it anyway.

Now if I'm doing what I don't want to do, it is plain to see where the trouble is because sin still has me in its evil grasp. At these times in your life where there's something in you that wants to do good, you're overwhelmed, you feel these feelings of frustration and you end up doing the very thing that you said you weren't going to do, didn't want to do again, but there we are right back doing it again; oh, that big, juicy doughnut is screaming my name, amen! Then you take a bite of it and feel discouragement and despair, more feelings, rotten feelings. Listen to verse 21; *it seems to be a fact of life that when I want to do what is right, I inevitably do what is wrong. In my mind I want to be God's willing servant, but instead I find myself still enslaved to sin.*

Hands On Freedom

There is freedom for you. If you can totally relate to what I've just said and you're feeling overwhelmed, maybe you're feeling discouraged, despair or hopelessness also. Those are emotions and feelings. Don't give up because there is freedom for you. Let me give you a little transition here, the thing about feelings is that our thinking often times leads to our feelings and then we take action. Let me tell you something, there are two ways to change your feelings. Feelings don't change feelings. Thinking changes feelings and actions change feelings. So you can attack feelings from both ways. God gave you your emotions and he gave you your feelings, but never, ever let your feelings tell you how to think and never let your feelings tell you how to act. Let your actions tell you how to feel and let your thinking tell you how to feel, but never let your feelings tell you how to think or how to act. Never let that sinner of feelings determine actions or thoughts...actions or thoughts. Make it go the other way...actions and thoughts rule feelings and emotions.

Let me tell you what people without Christ have. People without Christ have Tony Robbins, Oprah and Dr. Phil. You might say, *"I watched Oprah and she really helped me!"* and I would tell you that I love Oprah too. Tony Robbins, oh he's the man, I love Tony! Somebody say amen, Tony! Someone else may have read Dr. Phil's book. Let me share this with you: They have good stuff! You know what I've discovered from Oprah, Tony, Dr. Phil and you name your guy or gal? I've discovered that most of them are using biblical principles, but when you leave the power of God out of the equation, at best you are managing your willpower. I might be able to willpower my way away from that doughnut for a few days or a few hours or a few weeks but what you resist you will eventually attract. I will not eat that doughnut! I will not eat that doughnut! Or whatever it is, Doritos, or you know whatever you're trying not to do. I am naming my sins; I'm not trying to name yours.

The more you think about it, the more energy you give it. Pretty soon because you've thought about it and meditated on it, all of a sudden it has such power! It takes over and the next thing you know, it's in your mouth. Suddenly your self-talk changes again. *"I'm horrible; I'll never change! I thought this was my year; maybe it's next year."* Willpower! Motivational speakers like Tony Robbins have some good mental tricks for willpower. They explain how to change your focus, which is really a biblical principle. Yes, changing your focus is right out of the Bible. The Bible says resist the enemy. It doesn't say resist the doughnut; but what the Bible does say is how you resist the enemy. It says that you resist the enemy by refocusing your thoughts. Let me describe it this way; without Christ and without Jesus in the equation, here's what we do… Oprah, Tony, Dr. Phil…they take a pig that's in a muddy pig pen and they take it to the carwash and they hose it off. Then they take it and they put Oil of Olay on it. You know what I meant right? Olay! They lotion it up, put some perfume on it, tie a ribbon on it, put some lipstick on it, doctor it up. You can doctor that pig up all day long, fix it up, but let me tell you it's still a pig. It is still a pig!

When I choose the wild card, because you're all handed a card, it can be what you choose it to be; whatever you need. And when you choose the wild card of his spirit, let me tell you what happens. God gave you the ability to choose, you can choose to get healthy. This is your time. You should have no more of this self-talk of defeat. If you want to choose to get healthy, then say *"I will be healthy, I'm going to get healthy."*

Psalms 119:73 You made my body, now give me sense to heed your word or your law.

Lord let me heed and let me put your word first in my life.

See, what you are doing is this; you are detecting and disarming the lies that you believe. Because of the four things that I told you before, a lot of us have bought into them and a lot of you believe lies about yourselves. You know what believing a lie is? As far as you're concerned, it's true to you because you believe it. Even though it is not true; when you believe a lie, you've embraced it as truth and when you embrace something as true, you filter your life decisions and life choices through the fact that you think it's true even though it's not true. Did I just confuse you or are you with me? All right; behind every self-defeating act, behind every self-defeating action that I have, whatever I'm doing, behind every self-defeating act that I do is a lie believed. The truth is that you do have the power if you're in Christ. So to stop defeating yourself, you must stop deceiving yourself. You have to choose to say *"This is how I feel, I know I feel this way, yeah I ain't arguing with you."*

I had a young person tell me the other day that I didn't understand the way that they feel. But just because you feel that way does not mean that it is the truth. Because your feelings will lie to you, your feelings are fickle, your feelings go up and they go down and they're like a roller-coaster that spins all around. Your feelings are out of control… they're here then they're there. One minute you're like…Jesus! And the next minute you're like Jesus.

Kind of goes all over the place, doesn't it? How do you get free from this?

John 8:32 Then you'll know the truth and the truth is what will set you free.

Chapter 11
Re-Educate Your Mind

Do the one thing you think you cannot do. Fail at it. Try again. Do better the second time. The only people who never tumble are those who never mount the high wire. This is your moment. Own it. – Oprah Winfrey

So you have to re-educate your mind, that's what I'm getting at. I can choose what I think about. How do I do it? I re-educate my mind.

Romans 12:2 Let God transform you

What's transform? Change; a transformer changes voltage from this voltage to that voltage, you can voltage down or voltage up, transform down or transform up. Your mind can transform up or transform down too. When God's involved he's transforming you into his image. By the way, God is truth, he doesn't have a little bit of truth; he is the truth. He's the whole truth, he's nothing but the truth and so when we re-educate you, re-transform, let God transform you into a new person. How? By changing the way you think.

The key is to just let him do it. A lot of us think that he's just going to do it. We would like it if all that we had to do was say "God you know where I live. You know my address, 3303 Homer Adams Parkway, come and see me Jesus! Put the money in the mailbox too! And then change me, I don't want to have to do anything; you just change me, God. It doesn't work that way though. He requires cooperation with us. He wants us to cooperate with him and let God transform us into a new person by changing the way we think. You know, I'm surprised at how many Christians that I meet that are not willing to let go of old thought patterns that don't serve them well. They have believed a lie or they've believed tradition and it's not true at all, it's not the Bible. But many times we embrace those old thought patterns and those old traditions as being truth when they're not truth. We have all done it.

We all have to renew our mind, we all have to be re-educated with the word of God. When I choose the wild card of his spirit, I can have better thoughts. I really can, I can have better thoughts. In fact, that's one of the things that we need to say about ourselves.

"I can think better thoughts about myself, I can have good self-talk, I can because I'm an overcomer and in order for me to be a great overcomer I have to have the profile of an overcomer. I have to be able to have great self-talk."

When you set your mind on something, then who gets to choose? You do! YOU get to choose what you are going to set it on, so set it. When a concrete anchor is set, you drill a hole in that concrete, you set the anchor with a hammer and it's there. You ain't getting it out unless you chisel and break the concrete.

Romans 8:5 Those who live according to the sinful nature have their minds set on that nature's desire.

I want to encourage you to set the anchor of your mind here instead of within the world's philosophy, instead of maybe what mom and dad taught you, what the coach said about you, what you have said about yourself or even what your own DNA has said about you. You are letting God renew your mind. He said that those who live according to the spirit have their minds set on what the spirit desires. The mind of the sinful man is death, death means separation, but the mind controlled by the spirit of life is peace. How many of you need peace? I do, I love having peace of mind. That's valuable and the older I get, the more valuable it is. I love peace.

Romans 8:7 The sinful mind is hostile to God.

Do you know that I discovered that my flesh is hostile to God? Surprises you, doesn't it? It shouldn't surprise you, because all of us are that way. It all depends on how you feed your flesh nature.

It is dictated by what you think about. It's about whether or not you allow your mind to go down rabbit trails when something goes wrong. You could let your mind go and meditate on that thing that went wrong and think on it and dwell on it. When you do that you are giving attention to the mind of the flesh and that's hostile to God and God's ways. Those that are controlled by the sinful nature can't please God.

Romans 8:9 You, however, are not in the flesh but in the Spirit, if in fact the Spirit of God dwells in you. Anyone who does not have the Spirit of Christ does not belong to him.

I'm in this battle and you're in this battle. You do have the ability, we have the ability. When I say ability, I mean the power to say no more often. In verse 9, Paul is saying that you're different than that example, that you're controlled not by the sinful nature, but by the Spirit, capital "S", that means the Holy Spirit, if the Spirit of God lives in you. Does the Spirit of God live in you? Yes, he lives in you, and because he lives in you, you have something that Oprah can't give, with all of her great advice, biblical advice at that; Tony can't give and Dr. Phil can't give. Again, I think that these people are great. In fact, Tony and Oprah have become good friends with Joel Osteen recently, which is cool. It's neat how God's just doing his stuff and he brings the right people together. The factor that controls it is the wild card of the spirit of God living in you that unbelievers don't have. It's the power of God, the biblical back-up. All they have is willpower, sheer discipline and grit. You have the advantage because you have the power of the Spirit, the Holy Spirit living on the inside of you. I love that! So when you choose the wild card of the Spirit you can also choose Jesus as your Savior because all of us need a Savior. We don't just need a little like token salvation, we need complete salvation and Jesus is the way to that relationship.

2 Corinthians 5 He who has prepared us for this very thing is God, who has given us the Spirit as a guarantee.

I want you to get an image of this for you, because so many of us that are filled with his spirit and have him living in us, when I say filled with the Spirit, I mean you're saved, you're a Christian, you're a follower of Jesus Christ. Many of us still identify more with our old life than we do with the fact that we are Christians, followers of Jesus Christ and we are saved. Many of us have that old identity more so than we do with who we are in Christ.

Watch this, Paul said in 2 Corinthians 5:17, that when someone becomes a Christian, he or she becomes a new person on the inside. Your body doesn't get saved, that's why it still dies and gets sick and you have to fight and work out. But your spirit on the inside of you, you become a new person. He's not the same anymore, a new life has begun. There's power in you that you didn't have before.

When you choose the wild card of his spirit you realize, because you already were whether you realized it or not, that you are so valuable. What I'm talking about is if you're going to play out this overcomer of who you really are, you're going to have to realize that you're valuable. So many times we think that we're not valuable because we've compared our lives to others, because we've looked at others and we think that they do more, they have a bigger presence, a bigger platform, and they seem to be more effective. I want you to know something, that is self-talk that is self-defeating and that is a lie of the enemy. I don't care where you came from, where you're at in your process, what you've been through or what you have done or haven't done. You are so valuable, God chose you, God picked you to be born and that you are so special. I'm telling you that no one is an accident. God knew you would be born and you're valuable to him. You're special to him and he has a plan for your life. And though you might not see the full scope of what that plan is, I want you to know something, it's awesome and you have a piece to play in the role of what God's doing.

Did you know you're a co-laborer? What I love about Jesus; the Bible says that someday when this world wraps up (we should have eternity in mind right now) we'll be gone. If you live to be seventy, eighty or let's say you live to be one hundred years old; let's say you did that, did you realize that after one hundred and thirty years you'll be gone? You don't have that much time left. And you know what? It's better on that side. We're going to spend a thousand years on that side. A thousand times a million times a trillion times eternity and what I want you to know is when you pull back and you look at eternity, it's a lot easier to handle a little bit of trouble that you're going through today. Why is it that we focus, mentally focus, on the trouble and the struggle of one day or even one hour? We let it trip us out. Maybe we struggle with anger issues and blow up or whatever. You go eat. You go drink. You do whatever it is you do.

Why do you trip out on that instead of just deciding that you can handle a day of this, you can handle a week of this, you could really handle a year of this, for that matter, you could really handle a decade of this. Wait a minute, if you had to, you could handle a lifetime of this to get to the other side because, let me tell you something, once you get to the other side it's going to be awesome! The Bible says that you will share and you'll rule with Jesus. God has given you joint seating with Jesus Christ that you'll reign with him. The Bible says this! I don't know what that looks like, but maybe we'll each get a galaxy somewhere. I don't know how that works, but you'll rule and reign with him. It's kind of like Vegas. I've been there one time. Okay, in Vegas they have nothing to say but they sure know how to say it! Man, they know how to flash it and billboard it and video it…lights everywhere. So let's say Jesus is starring in Vegas and you're driving down the road and you see, **"Starring in today's performance, Jesus, co-starring your name in eternity."**

Because you're so important and you're so valuable to him, that he picked you to be his partner and you say surely that couldn't be true. You may still believe that you are not worthy and that surely couldn't be true because you have behaved so badly. Surely it's not true because you don't have the skill sets and the talents. I want you to know something, God knew you. He's not disappointed by the way you are. He reminds you that "*I knew it before, I knew it before, I loved him, I could have squashed you a long time ago, I didn't squash you. I love you and I picked you.*" He is telling you that there's still hope for you. It's not over, no! Your best days are ahead of you, but I'm giving you a free will, and here's the wildcard. You got dealt a wildcard. I want to encourage you to realize that you're valuable.

1 Peter 2:9 But you are a chosen people, a royal priesthood, a holy nation, God's special possession, that you may declare the praises of him who called you out of darkness into his wonderful light.

You have been chosen by God himself, he picked you. You're a priest of the King, you're holy and you're pure and you're God's very own. You're his possession. You're his prize and you belong to him. He owns you! You're God's very own! He is telling you all of this so that you may show to others how God called you out of the darkness into his marvelous light. Here's what you're supposed to realize: he owns you because he called you out of darkness and the fact that when you realize you're precious to him and he owns you. The whole purpose of it is for you to be a testimony of his goodness. Here's a testimony of one of the multitudes who were dark and hopeless at one time, they were far from God, but now they're in the light. They're in the light.

Deuteronomy 7:6 For you are a people holy to the Lord your God. The Lord your God has chosen you out of all the peoples on the face of the earth to be his people, his treasured possession.

It says that you're a people wholly to the Lord. You are his treasure…you're his treasured possession. In other words, I don't know if you have anything that's so precious to you that you would it would be unbearable to lose, but that's what you are to God. You're so precious to him it would be unbearable to lose you. So here's what I want to say, have some sound self-talk. You need to be able to remember that you are forgiven. There is now no condemnation for those who are in Christ Jesus. Are you with me?

Isaiah 43:25 I am the God who forgives your sins. I do this because of who I am; I will not hold your sins against you.

And then you need to say those things about yourself instead of saying "*I don't know if I can do it.*" You need to say "*I am capable; it's biblical.*"

2 Corinthians 3:5 The capacity we have comes from God and it is he who has made us capable of serving the new covenant.

You're capable!

Philippians 4:13, I can do everything, all things through Christ Jesus that gives me strength.

Self-talk; let the weak say I am strong, let the poor say I am rich. *This message is encompassing, this message includes every person. You're an overcomer, you are overcomers, I declare over you, it's your time, it's your destiny, this is the hour of your breakthrough.*

This is the hour for you to realize who you are in Jesus, for you to be free from the bondage of self-condemnation and negative talk about yourself, to realize that you're beautiful, that you're who God made and that his love for you is never ending. That your sins are forgiven, that there is hope for a great future and that the power of God is on the inside of the you to say no, the power of God is on the inside of you to choose your actions, the power of God is on the inside of you to choose the way you think and though feelings may lie and come and go and try to whip you around.

You're in control and you're setting your mind and you're setting your heart on God and on his word and putting him first. So I declare over you this day you are free in Jesus' name. I declare you are free and you are blessed.

Chapter 12
Compounding Breakthrough

"The soul grows into lovely habits as easily as into ugly ones, and the moment a life begins to blossom into beautiful words and deeds, that moment a new standard of conduct is established, and your eager neighbors look to you for a continuous manifestation of the good cheer, the sympathy, the ready wit, the comradeship, or the inspiration, you once showed yourself capable of. Bear figs for a season or two, and the world outside the orchard is very unwilling you should bear thistles." - Kate Douglas Wiggin, Rebecca of Sunnybrook Farm

In the previous chapters, we talked about what an overcomer looks like. One of the profiles of an overcomer is that an overcomer has stellar habits. And what I mean by that is disciplines. You know, we call Christians disciples. It means a disciplined one and for us to be disciplined ones, disciples, people that have great habits; in other words, if I could bring it up to modern language, just good old fashioned healthy habits. Doing the right thing day after day, that brings success.

Mathew 11:19, Jesus came to enjoy life.

Now it's funny that he came enjoying life because he knew what he was here to do. He was here to pay for our sins. I don't know if I was here to pay for your sins, if I would enjoy my life. Would you? But he came enjoying life. I love that. Why did he do that? Because he set the example for us, he said it again in John 10:10, *"I came that you might have life, have it in abundance; to the full till it overflows and I believe that."*

The Anatomy Of A Habit

I want to talk about the anatomy, or the DNA of what a habit is and how a habit gets formed. Do you know that you can have good habits and you can have bad habits? You've got a few good ones don't you? And probably have some bad ones too. We all are working out the bad ones, releasing and letting go of those bad ones, and we're trying to pick up the good ones and develop those.

Deuteronomy 28:63 The Lord is happy to make you successful and to help your nation grow while you conquer the land.

So here's my prayer for you: God has an agenda for you, God has an assignment for you, God has a plan and a purpose for your life and that is to conquer and to overcome. The first thing that he told Adam and Eve was be fruitful and multiply, go out and conquer, go out and occupy, and that's what he wants you to do. He does not want you to just sit on the couch and be a potato. He wants you to get out and live life. Live your life, enjoy life! You will have opposition in this world and there will be trouble, but be of good cheer for I have overcome the world for you on your behalf so good news, good news, good news.

Yes, there's opposition and yes, you're going to face some obstacles, but the good news is that he's overcome and if we don't quit, if we stay in the game, we win in the end. And so I want to teach you how to develop these good habits because there's a payoff. Did you know there's even a payoff for your bad habits? I often ask people why they do what they do. You know, somebody will tell me that they were struggling with something. They were whining and crying and I ask them what the payoff is. Usually they are insulted that I said there's a payoff for that. No, there's always a payoff for every habit, even if it's a bad one, there's a payoff. If we are objective enough, we realize that. Objective means you can pull back and you can look at it and go objectively, *"Yeah I'm jacked up! I'm messed up."* At least be honest enough to say, *"Well, here's my payoff."* I do this because I get sympathy; I do this because this meets a need in my flesh. See, the payoff for a familiar habit is often times that familiarity that we get accustomed to.

The problem with most habits is that when we develop a habit; a bad habit or sometimes even a good habit, often times because of those habits we identify and get our identity from what we have done. Not who we are. That's what I'm all about, is bringing you the revelation of the truth of God's word that says that you are transformed and you are changed by the renewing of your mind, by the way you think, so you've got to think different. Here's the problem, if you go on auto-pilot, and the truth is that a lot of us do go on auto-pilot for our lives, even Christians… Christ-followers…a lot of times we just live this life on auto-pilot without having renewed the mind to challenge the old self.

Romans Chapter 7 talks about how we do things that we don't want to do. *"Oh man, I end up doing this thing I don't want to do. I don't want to do it and I end up doing it."* It's usually a bad habit that you've become addicted to, it's the flesh though. It's your flesh, my flesh. But Romans Chapter 8 teaches us how to live by the Spirit of God; how to get the revelation of his spirit to be empowered so that you can get your power from the spirit of God. I want to talk about that; the word familiar. Most of us are familiar with our surroundings. We're familiar with the way we grew up, with our habits. The word familiar means *from that of family.* So it's like it comes from our family, it comes from the family that we have. Habits kind of give us a little bit of our identity. You've heard it said, *"I am Daren and I am an alcoholic."* What are we doing? We're identifying our self; we got our identity from our old habit. I'm just saying to you, a lot of times it's the habit that we participate in and/or don't participate in, that we identify with. *"Hi, I'm Daren, I'm shy. Hi, I'm Daren, I'm unorganized. Hi, I'm Daren, I'm crazy."*

It may be habits that you have done or the actions that you have taken that you embrace as your identity. That is not your identity, but often times we receive it as our identity. There is power in a habit. I'm going to break down a habit, what a habit is and I am going to give you the DNA of a habit. There is power in habits. If you want to change your life, change what you do daily, I'm telling you to make it a habit. Change what you do, in a positive way, on a daily basis and you will change your life. And likewise, it goes the other way, if you want to change your life for the negative, just change a few things. It's okay to eat a doughnut or something unhealthy every once in a while, but if you do it every day, all day long, how many of you know you just won't live quite as long? You just won't, I mean you still go to heaven; you just get there a lot quicker!

1 Timothy 4:7 Take the time and the trouble to keep yourself spiritually fit.

A habit will create momentum. I am talking about discipline. I am talking about you being the overcomer that you are and I want to encourage you to do the things that keep you spiritually fit. Don't let yourself go flabby spiritually. Bodily exercise or physical exercise, the scripture goes on and says it profits a little. But spiritual exercise we all need to be participating in. We need to get buff spiritually. I really encourage you to take the time to do that. Get yoked out with the yoke. Make it your habit. Have your senses exercised for distinguishing both good and evil. You have empowering habits and you have disempowering habits. Some habits give you momentum and some habits give you power to live a better life, to live a better day, to be a better person, to be a better husband, to be a better wife, to be a better parent, a better worker or a better employer.

Disempowering The Vandalism Of Baby Food

Hebrews 5:14 Solid food belongs to the full grown man.

That applies to women too. You're grown up, so you should eat solid food. So what should be happening in your life is that you are growing up spiritually, you are exercising spiritually, you get spiritually fit and you are learning what is good and bad for you. You learn to say yes to things and no to others so that you grow spiritually. Are you with me? I'm encouraging you because you're an overcomer. I'm just encouraging you! You're an overcomer, yes you are, you're a conqueror, you're a winner, you're a champion, you can defeat the enemy and you're a winner!

Proverbs 18:9 Slack habit and sloppy work are as bad as vandalism.

How many of you like things to be vandalized? Don't you detest it? Have you ever had anything vandalized? It's just a horrible feeling, isn't it? Thank God for insurance! If you make statements like *"I don't know how this always happens to me,"* let me just tell you that's a disempowering habit. You cannot walk around dogging yourself all of the time. If someone tells you that you look good then take that compliment. Don't think that they were just being nice, or that you don't really look good. Say thank you and believe it. Say thank you, thank you amen!

Here is another disempowering habit. Did you ever end up at the drive through window and you don't know how you got there? You're not even hungry, but that chocolate malt just sounded good. It's Friday; and you always have chocolate malts on Friday. It's simply a bad habit. Did you ever eat something and you think to yourself that you don't know why you ate it? You are sitting there and you have no idea why. You were full, but it was there and it looked good, so you ate it. That's a disempowering habit. Habits either serve you or they don't serve you and it is spiritual for us to talk about habits. It is when it relates to us letting go of some of those habits that are not for the kingdom.

I'll tell you a big habit that's a bad one for a lot of us. We haven't even identified it yet… procrastination. Yeah, it's a big one! Typically, the cause of procrastination is usually being overwhelmed. You don't wake up and just think that you are going to procrastinate that particular day. You don't want to put a bunch of stuff off today. No, nobody does that. Procrastination usually happens as a by-product of things that you wanted to get done but you are so overwhelmed with not knowing where to start that you just put it off for another hour. Maybe you put it off for two hours or a day or a week or a month or a year or ten years. Yes, sometimes we can't get our cars in our garage for ten years.

Father Forgive Me, For I Have Sinned

Confession is good for the soul. Confess to God and ask him to forgive you. Tell him that you have sinned by not cleaning out your garage or closet or even just a messy drawer for ten years. Yes, procrastination can turn into a sin. These are the types of things that are disempowering habits because when there's clutter it will affect your spiritual condition. When you're cleaned up and I don't mean you have to be a freak about it, but when you clean up a little bit and you get things a little bit organized, did you know that your head is better? Your soul is better, your spirit functions better? Bad habits are there when we just wing it or we put things off. Even worse than just putting those things off, is the bad habit of living in denial. You will convince yourself that you don't have a problem and everybody else knows that you do!

I've got a person like that in my life right now that I'm talking with. I've tried to explain that the situation is out of hand and the only response that I get is, *"No I don't, no I don't, no I don't."* Denial! Did you know you can't help someone until they admit it? Until they admit that they've got a problem and need some help with it. Once you get them to that place, then you can get help for them; that's a good thing isn't it?

Chapter 13
Broke-down Habits

"The last three or four reps is what makes the muscle grow. This area of pain divides the champion from someone else who is not a champion. That's what most people lack, having the guts to go on and just say they'll go through the pain no matter what happens." - *Arnold Schwarzenegger*

So, let me tell you the DNA of a habit and how it's developed. Typically, it's developed through a few things. You have to tell God what you want cleaned up in your life. Ask Him to search you, to help you out there, to help you know your heart and test you by knowing your anxious thoughts. Pray. Ask God to lead you in the way of the everlasting. You must get your heart pure through a prayer to God by saying *"God I'm going to need your help, I'm going to need your direction. I'm going to need you here to help me. If I've got some offense going on am I self-deceived in some areas here, I need a little bit of help Jesus, help me out."*

Psalms 139 Search me oh God and know my heart.

Let me tell you how habits are developed, good ones and bad ones, and how they come into your life. The first way and often times a very powerful way is through generational transfer. A lot of Bible teachers call it the generational curse. But there's also a generational blessing that you can pass down too, which by the way, I would encourage you to do since you are overcomers and conquerors! Pass down the blessing to your children and to your children's children. Pass it down, begin to declare over them when they're little babies and as they grow up, *you are blessed, you are favored; you have favor.* We do that every day on the way to school with our kids and we've done that through the years. Cassidy's the last of our children left in school and we speak that over her every morning. *"You are blessed and you have favor with all your teachers and you have favor with students and favor everywhere you go, favor, favor, favor, you're blessed Cassidy! We speak the generational blessing on you and may it even multiply on you."* And it should get stronger with each generation.

A Curse And A Blessing

There are also generational curses or inequities, the Bible calls them inequities. What does that mean? Well you've seen those things where for generations there was poverty, for generation's poverty, poverty, poverty, poverty, poverty, or sexual addiction, sexual abuse, sexual abuse, a pornography addiction passed down, passed down.

Promiscuity, generations in a family getting pregnant way before they're married. Alcoholism or other sins also get passed down. Anger issues; *"Oh I'm just angry, don't think anything about it, that's the way my Grandpa was, Great-Grandpa was angry and I'm angry too. I'm just like all them."* What is that? That's generational transfer. The Bible calls it inequities that get passed down to us.

Here's another one, events. How many of you know when an event happens on the playground or on the sports field with a coach or with a parent, an abuse situation could take place, it's an event that helps create an identity? Maybe you were abandoned and you never knew your father. Let me tell you, typically when that happens, you have abandonment issues and embrace that as part of your identity. You embrace that you have issues with that and you just trip everything over being abandoned or being hurt or being raped or being abused, are you with me? Feelings are another thing. I've taught you that feelings are neutral. Feelings are conditions that create moods that create behaviors. For example, you can have a feeling that's a good feeling or a bad feeling. You can also do something that creates a feeling. How many of you know sin is pleasurable for a moment, for a season but then in the end it brings sin? How many of you know in that moment of pleasure, a feeling or a mood happened and you identified with that and you hooked up with that and now you have a hard time releasing and letting go of that feeling and that buzz that you found in that sinful moment.

It can go the other way and you can use that for the positive too though. Like during praise and worship. It has a mood, a feeling, it has an emotion and what I would encourage you to do is to get addicted to that environment, that way you don't miss church and you press in for more church and for more of God, are you with me?

Repetition and practice creates the neurons in our brain that wire and fire. That is why habits are so powerful in our life.

Scientific Habits

Now I love science, I may have mentioned it before once or twice. Science was one of my favorite subjects in school and it still is. I love science because science and faith blend so perfectly. It's funny how secular humanists think that science and faith are so far apart, as if God is in heaven wondering what to do with science. He's the father of science, come on, he invented everything; atoms and neutrons, blood vessels and dinosaurs, clouds, sky and gravity. God invented all of that, so science is not a surprise to God. Your brain has neurons that fire and that wire to create circuitry and when you repeat something and you practice it over and over, those wires remember. Have you ever smoked? If you have, I bet you also remember the first time you smoked a cigarette and how horrible that was. What about those of you who have ever tried chewing tobacco? Do you remember the first time you chewed tobacco and you turned green? Even a person's first sip of alcohol is horrendous.

And then what'd you do? You went back and practiced again and you repeated it and you rewired the wiring, the hardware up in the circuitry of your brain and all of a sudden the thing that you were grossed out on you could do.

That hard wiring happens in a negative way, but I want you to know something, it works the other way too. When you begin to work out with weights and you begin to exercise something happens too. They call it the runner's high, it's endorphins that begin to release and you get a buzz from exercising. When you rewire serving God and practice reading your Bible daily, praying and worshipping, lifting your hands, your mind gets used to it, it becomes a normal habit.

When I first came into church and people were raising their hands, I came from a background where we did not do that, it was weird to me. I thought that those people were nuts. I was like man, they're just like raising their hands and they were into church and no matter how weird and uncomfortable it was for me, there was a part of me that found it to be intriguing, but I wasn't going to become one of them. But I did want to be around it a little more because it was somehow *familiar*. Let me tell you what happened…I did it and everybody in the church turned and went he did it! He raised his hand! No, they didn't do that but that's what I thought they were going to do. Do you know how narcissistic that must be for me to think that way? I'm a narcissist I guess, because I thought I'm raising my hand, everybody there probably knew I raised my hand. We're so self-centered aren't we? Everybody's thinking about themselves; they're not thinking about you.

I pictured them having prayer meetings, let's pray, this is his fourth time at church, let's pray that tonight's the night he gets breakthrough and he'll raise his hands tonight. Here's what happened, I raised my hand a little bit, it was pretty easy, it didn't require that much. I did it and nobody tripped out on it. Nobody whispered, *"Oh he's raised his hand!"* Nobody did that! They just acted like it was normal. So the next time I raised it little bit further and pretty soon I was raising my hands all the way and nobody acknowledged it! It just showed me that I didn't matter, you know? Through practice and repetition now I can do it, and not only that, when the music's jamming I can even bounce a little bit and I can jam to it because here's the truth: I'm a fan!

I'm a fan of the Cardinals, the Blues, the Rams and a few other teams. I'm a fan and I'm a fan at those games. If you see me at a game I'm whistling and hollering and I'm thinking to myself, Jesus is the center of it all, why would I be tame, lame, and held back? Why would I be a woos? Yes, and I said that word on purpose, why would I woos out in my praise and worship?

I mean if I'm going to do that for a baseball team, I'm going to do it for the one that saved my soul that loves me. So I'm going to practice.

Practice Makes Perfect

You must understand the cause and the effect of your habits. Did you know there is a cause that makes you do things and that is why you need to go deep with this a little bit? I'm not going to go deep, but I want you to take this outline and I want you to get with God, get alone with Him, get a little bit of prayer time and say God what causes me to continue to repeat this in my life. *"Why is it that I keep coming back around to this issue that I'm dealing with?"* And you know what it is; we've all got it okay? What is it? What is it?

Psalms 119:73 God you made me, you made my body, Lord give me the sense to heed your word. God give me the ability to take your word and ask why I keep coming around.
Some of us were more successful when we weren't with God. You come to God and all of a sudden you struggle. Breakthrough…you need breakthrough! God is concerned with the outcome of you. He prepared a plan and path for you and he's concerned with you fulfilling your destiny that he has for you. And here's the thing about God, he's oh so patient. He is so patient! Now sometimes I wish he'd get in a hurry and just make me become that person! But he is patient with me because I have a free will like you, and he's working with us to become that person.

So how do we change it? Well we have to change our thoughts about the event that took place. A lot of us have attached a meaning to this event. I was abandoned, I was raped, I was fired, I was passed over for a promotion. I was always the last one to be picked for the team in grade school, whatever. And so we have these events that we've attached meaning to, we've attached our identity to and we have got to change our thoughts about those and quit embracing the old, meaningless lies of the devil. The devil has lied to us and we have to let that go.

1 Peter 1:6 Now though for a little we've had to suffer grief and all kinds of trials, these have come so that our faith of greater worth than gold which perishes even though it is refined by fire, may be proved genuine and may result in praise, glory, honor, when Jesus Christ is revealed.

Here's what I want you to do: change your attitude, change your view. Maybe your mom or your dad didn't want anything to do with you; maybe they did horrible things to you. You were passed over, laid off, it's horrible. She walked out the door, he walked out the door. Let that be the thing that God uses to build your life! Instead of looking at it as like this horrible thing that happened to you; now look at it and remember that yes, I know it was horrible, but you are here because God wants you here. Remember that He is God and because your faith is being developed you can now realize that what the devil meant for harm, God's going to turn around. Though the devil tried to bring you down, to ruin your life and to take a child away from God, you have the ability to conquer him and return to the destiny that God so desperately wants you to embrace. Let's turn it around! Turn your thinking about it around and let God use it to just beat the stuff out of the devil! Change your thinking about it.

Release And Let Go

Learn to release and let go. A lot of times people white knuckle their addictions. *"I'm going to quit smoking, I'm going to quit smoking, I'm going to quit thinking about whatever, I'm going to quit, I'm going to quit."* Your grasp grows tighter and tighter and your fist gets whiter but eventually it will give out. We white knuckle it. I want you to know you've got to breathe deep, release, cast all of your cares on God for he cares for you.

Here's another one, did you know we all have attitudes about money? For the most part it was imparted to us from our parents or those that we grew up around. Did you know that? We have an opinion about money, an idea about money; and it's a direct reflection of the circle of influence that we came. Some people think that money is just down right evil and they have a hard time with it. Some people have said money is the root of all evil and that is just not true. The love of money is…the love of money is. Some people have an attitude, a viewpoint about money and how hard it is to get and how hard it is to keep. Money is elusive and it's hard to earn. If you have those ideas or those opinions about money I want to challenge you in the name of Jesus to let those ideas and those opinions about money go. It is false and it is a lie of the enemy to keep you in a position of lack where there's not enough.

God wants you to have enough; I'm not saying he wants you to drive a Rolls-Royce or a Bentley, but what he does want is that you to have enough to pay your electric bill and if an appliance breaks down you can buy a new one. If your neighbor needs help, you can help them. That is when you are wealthy. If I've got an opinion about money and we think that it's hard to get and you can't keep it, remember that God is the God of abundance and he owns everything. He's my Daddy, I'm his kid, there ought to not be lack in my life and I need to retrain my mind with that.

What Are Those Feelings?

Understand feelings for what they are. I've told you this before and it is a big concept. You will grow up if you identify feelings.

Feelings and emotions, they're good when they're good and they're bad when they're bad, but a feeling can't change a feeling. I can't be feeling bad and just go hey, happy feeling come in and change it. But let me tell you, the two things that will change a feeling are thoughts and follow up. Change the way that you think. You've got to pull back, change your angle, instead of looking at it the way you are, you have got to pull back. It's hard to do, and it takes maturity to do this. You have got to pull back and decide that you are going to look at this thing differently. But then you have to follow it up. These are the things that attack a feeling to change it. You have to follow it up with an action. You have got to do something, in fact, doing something will change it.

James 1:21 Get rid of every filthy habit and all wicked conduct. Submit to God and accept the word that he plants in your heart, this word is able to save you.

Save you from what? Save you from horrible feelings, self-deprecation, resentment, anger. How am I going to break the habits? The Bible just gave you the key. You have to submit, you have to say *"Okay, I pulled back I submit, God help me think different, help me view this different; I'm going to…I've looked at it this way for thirty years, but it's a new day. I've been sitting in church, I've been renewing my mind with the word of God, I'm going to pull back and believe your word Lord. I'm going to believe what that pastor said and what your word says, I'm going to believe it, I'm going to embrace it and I'm going to attack that thing with a different attitude and with a new action."*

Get Buzzed!

Ephesians 3:18 May you be able to feel.

Your feelings are okay and may you be able to understand and experience God's love for yourself. We exist to lead people to experience and to enjoy a God-first life. Did you know there's a feeling that comes with living a God-first life? It's a buzz! You can get a better buzz than drugs, you can get a better buzz than substance; you can get the buzz of the Holy Spirit by serving him and living for him. So if you're dealing with feelings of being overwhelmed and you've got these disempowering habits, your bodies and the chemicals in your body begin to actually create a feeling and release chemicals. Did you know that? This is the science blending with the faith. If you get overwhelmed and the chemicals start releasing, I want to challenge you to physically change the way you feel. It's time to begin to think different, stop a feeling in its tracks with an action You talk about a buzz, go through a drive-thru and pay for the meal behind you and if it's too much for you, just go through the drive-thru again, a second time, you'll get somebody you can afford. I promise you. Pay for their meal, you just served somebody, but you're the one with the buzz.

You need a buzz? Then go serve somebody, go take an action, volunteer, get behind a camera, be a greeter, volunteer. Your thoughts can change your feelings; your actions can change a feeling. Next, to keep that buzz, you must learn to practice forgiveness. Let go of hurt and pain. Let go of disappointment. You can't move forward without forgiveness. Love knows no limits, it endures to the end, no fading of hope; it can outlast anything. Love is the champion, love is the winner. It's the key to everything. Did you know even your faith works by your love? So you've got to release, you've got to let go. You can't release your habits if you won't forgive, so you've got to forgive. You've got to have a systematic approach. You have to release what disempowers you and create empowering habits through a system.

This is why the twelve step program has worked so successfully for so long, because it is a system of accountability. You have to have a system.

Nehemiah 9:39 We are making a binding agreement, printing it, writing it down, our spiritual leaders are affixing their seal to it.

So what is this? This is called accountability. This is where you commit to something, whether it is serving the church, the community or some other area. You will be accountable to those that you commit to and they will expect nothing but the best from you. The twelve step program works because it has a system, you start going to a meeting. Did you know in the beginning sometimes you go to a meeting once a day, sometimes twice a day, if you're really, really hooked and you need help, you go three times a day! What do you do? You have an accountability partner you hook up with them. You connect, this is why it works, there's accountability, there's a system, twelve step system, come on, so if it works so well in the natural, and by the way that twelve step program is pretty much biblically based for the most part, if it works that way shouldn't we in the church have an even stronger foundational system?

Did you know that what you focus on you attract? And the mistake most of us make is that white knuckle process; we white knuckle our addictions. I'm going to quit smoking, and what do we do? We think about a cigarette all day long. I'm going to quit, I'm going to quit and then a doughnut or whatever it is, pornography, whatever, you name it, it's your deal. You're white knuckling it. I'm going to quit, I'm going to quit, but what you focus on you attract.

Let me give you a couple of examples. I talked to a racecar driver that was driving over two hundred miles an hour, inches from the wall. Someone asked him how he keeps from hitting the wall? He said that he never looks at the wall. If you look at the wall, you will hit the wall. Let me just tell you that what you focus on, what you look at, you will hit. So what do you do? You have to replace it. Quit looking at the thing, the Proverbs says it this way; don't go by the prostitutes house. Don't go by and look. So what do you do? How do you it? Do you remember Sonny and Cher? Sonny Bono, remember Sonny? Do you know he was a great snow skier? Did you know he hit a tree while skiing? Did you know why he hit the tree? He looked at the tree; he lost his focus on the space. I know it's an accident, yes, but ask great skiers how they miss the trees. They will tell you that they don't ever focus on the tree, but instead they focus on the space.

It is a biblical principle. The reason a lot of us create this anxiety in our heart towards being overwhelmed is because we look at our problems and focus on the problems. We white knuckle our addictions, we white knuckle our problems. You must decide to focus on the solution. I'm going to focus on the enjoyment of loving God, coming to church, the bills, the bills, the bills, ahhhh the bills, I'm going to focus on the Lord of the bills. Are you with me? And then practice your daily spiritual, emotional and physical discipline, one day at a time. This is a one day at a time system. It is one day at a time, it takes a life time; it takes several seasons to hit the Hall of Fame. You don't hit the Hall of Fame in one season. You are in a marathon, not a sprint.

Finally, remember all actions contain seeds that grow a harvest. This is why activity is so wonderful. You can never feel your way into an action, but you can act your way into a feeling. Marriages that are suffering and hurting, this is a great thing you can do, wife you don't have any feelings for your husband…act like you do. Really! You know it works the other way men too! There you go ladies! You can act your way into a feeling. You start talking about how handsome he is and how good looking he is and how beautiful she is and how much you love the way she looks and her shape. I'm just telling you right now that there is a process of action that has seeds in it.

Now here's the good thing about it, know this, that when you plant a seed into the ground it has a harvest. You may not feel it when you act like you like him or act like you like her. You may not feel anything yet, but keep on acting. Because every action, every meal you buy at a restaurant, every time you pay for someone's gas, every time you serve; there are seeds going into the ground that's going to produce a harvest. All of a sudden, you won't know when it happened, you'll just scratch your head and remember when you used to feel nothing and all of a sudden your spouse is the apple of your eye. *"I am so in love with you, I want to just kiss you all over right now,"* and all of a sudden it's not fake feelings anymore, those are the real deal.

You fell back in love, but you can't feel your way into an action, you've got to think an action, take an action and it'll happen. Come on!

2 Corinthians 4:16 The reason we never lose heart, our body does indeed suffer and wears out, but every day the inward man receives fresh strength.

Chapter 14
Student of the Game

Ever tried? Ever failed? No matter. Try Again. Fail again. Fail better. - Samuel Beckett

At this point, you should be ready to start your journey as an Overcomer. I want to conclude this book with the profile of being a student of the game, or in other words for us as Christ followers, we are overcomers because we have faith and our faith increases and we study our faith. Anybody that's successful in anything, anybody that becomes a Hall of Famer, anyone who becomes great in their prospective field; become great because they study and they learn and they are constantly a student of the game. There is a guitar player at my church named Eric. I talk to him from time to time and he just practices, he's been playing guitar for years, but he practices guitar for hours upon hours every day and that's why he plays the way he does. I want to encourage you in your walk with Christ to study what other people of faith do and how they live their lives. Study the word and when you see someone do something great, they overcome an obstacle, a hurdle, a sickness or they have great adversity that comes against them, study what they do, study the word, and be encouraged by one another.

2 Timothy 2:15 Study and be eager to do your utmost, that's your best, to present yourself to God, approved, tested by trial, a workman.

We are workmen aren't we? We're workers, not couch potato people. We're not observers from the grandstands, we're in the game. There is a big difference there. A lot of people are spectators. They like to watch other people live life and do great things. The real fun of living life is when you get in the game, when you take the risk, when you run with the ball and you get the hit. *A workman has no cause to be ashamed.* Why do you have no cause to be ashamed? You're in the game, because you're going for it. Correctly analyzing and accurately dividing, rightly handling and skillfully teaching the word of truth.

Joshua said to meditate on it day and night so that you'll be sure to obey everything that's in it. Only then will you prosper and succeed in all that you do. The book of Joshua is a great starting point for your continuance of practice. I want you to fully understand that God does care about your success. He does want you to prosper in your life. He wants you to overcome the hurdles and the obstacles in life. You're an overcomer, he says you're more than a conqueror, he says you're a winner, you're a champion and I want to remind you of who you are in Christ!

The way you're going to renew your mind and change your self-talk is to change your old viewpoint and your old habits of the way you use to do life, the way you've always done things before. Become uncomfortable. Maybe you've always had a lack mentality or maybe you've always been defeated. You've always viewed yourself that way and I want you to know something, by renewing yourself and studying the word of God, you'll change your self image, you'll change your self-talk, you'll change the picture of who you are and you'll line up with Christ and who he says that you are. You've got to study the word and meditate on the word.

1 Chronicles 16:11 Study God and his strength and seek him day and night.

You'll never be ashamed when you study the Lord.

Matthew 17:20 If you have faith as small as a mustard seed you can say to this mountain move from here to there and it will move. Nothing will be impossible for you.

Say it. *"**Nothing will be impossible for me!**"* Part of the profile of an overcomer is that you're a dreamer, that you have vision; that you look forward, that you go forward, and that you move forward. You've got your eye on something, you don't just live haphazardly from day to day, but you're going for it.

Something is stirring in your heart. Do you remember the profile of passion? Having a big heart, a heart that expands with passion for what God has called you to do on this planet is an amazing gift. Why is faith so important? Well it's very important for us as Christ followers. We need to develop our faith, nurture and feed it and not let it just be there, but to develop and grow your faith to be an overcomer.

2 Corinthians 13:5 Examine yourself well, the scripture says examine to see whether you are in faith.

Examine yourself… stop and exam yourself. Hopefully you did this, you got up and you went and looked in the mirror and you examined yourself. I always get food on my teeth when I eat and people that love me will tell me, but those that don't, they just laugh. Examine yourself well, the scripture says examine to see whether you are in faith. Examine yourself, am I in faith really?

I think it's wise for us to stop for a few minutes and to examine our self and to see if we really are in faith. It goes on and says *"don't you realize that Christ is in you?"* A lot of us think we're overcomers because we've got that fish symbol on the back of our car. I'm an overcomer! Yeah, I drove past a car that had the fish symbol and I saw him give the one finger salute to another car twice. You are not a Christian and an Overcomer just because you have the right bumper sticker or because you gave money at Wal-Mart to the fundraiser that was out front.

Isn't it funny though, that when you talk to a lot of people, they attach their Christianity and they attach their faith to their deeds? They think they have faith because they had the faith to put a fish or a bumper sticker on their car. They gave at a fundraiser and so therefore I'm a good person. I must be a Christian. And that's why I encourage you to stop and examine yourself to see if you are. How important is your faith? Did you know your salvation is received through your faith? It says in Ephesians *"for it is by the grace of God,"* it's not that you're doing it, but that you've been saved through faith. You have to believe it. It's the receiving; the faith is the unwrapping and the opening of the gift that God has given you. It's not a result of your own effort, but it's a gift of God so that no one can boast about it. Are you with me?

I preach big dreams and often I have to be careful of what I preach here because we've got some people that will believe it right? I preached a message called NSD, No Small Dreams, and the drummer at my church, Matt, he comes in the week after I preached the message No Small Dreams and he pulls his shirt up. Boom! He had tattooed NSD, No Small Dreams, right there, it was right there on a tattoo. You know the Bible even tells that our faith actually limits what God has the ability to do in our life.

Now that's mind boggling.

Matthew 13:58 Jesus did not do many works of power in his own home town because of their unbelief and lack of faith.

Wow! Faith determines what God can do in your life.

Matthew 9:27 Jesus said, become what you believe.

Become what you believe. Faith has a posture. Faith has an attitude. Faith has a disposition. It has a feel, it has an air; it has a confidence, an expectation. A while back a family in my church wrote me a letter and in the letter they explained that they were having a very difficult time, they were having a hard time financially and they went on and talked about that a little bit, but it was the most amazing thing because they didn't ask for anything. In fact, in the letter was a check for two hundred dollars to Enjoy Church that said this, *"Please use this as a seed because we need a harvest."*

They didn't complain, they just told me where they were at and why they were doing what they were doing. They said that they knew that the principle of faith says that you can't out give God and that if they need this harvest then they needed to get some extra seed in the ground. They asked me to use it to reach some people who are hurting and who are broken. Now that's what I'm talking about when I say faith determines what God can do in my life. It's one thing to say you have faith. It's one thing to shout we're winners, we're champions! But it's another thing to get out on the court, to get out on the field and to live and play in the game of life.

I call it a game, it's not really a game you know but the Bible does and Paul referred to it many times in the scripture as an athletic event, as a run, as a race, as a boxing match, as a fight and so I just encourage you stay in there. Jesus said it again in Matthew 9:29

"According to your faith it'll be done to you." So it's kind of like you get to choose. There are over seven thousand promises in this word and your faith is the key that unlocks those promises of God in your life. You're an overcomer, you're a winner; you're a champion! I am encouraging you because you're a winner and we've talked a lot in this book about the Hall of Famers and how they don't typically get in the Hall of Fame through one season. It takes many seasons of discipline and consistency. Do you know that the book of Acts is still being written? I see many of you as someday having your story being told somewhere in the eternities. A story of how you lived by faith and you overcame great obstacles and you stayed in the game and you didn't quit and you went for it and you believed God. Someday you'll be in the Hall of Fame of faith, I believe that.

Hebrews 11:1 Faith that assures us of the things we expect and convinces of the existence of the things that we do not see.

Overcomer faith is choosing and believing God's dream for your life. I've discovered in my own life that God's dream for my life is much different and much bigger than my own dream. Often times I end up in God's court doing things that I never thought I had the ability to do. I want you to know something, if you can do it on your own and you don't need God, then it's not a good dream. You need a dream and you need a challenge that you will definitely fail at if you don't have God doing his part in your life; so I encourage you. Where there is no vision the people perish.

Ephesians 3:20 God by his mighty power at work within us is able to do far more than we could ever dare ask, even dream of, infinitely beyond our highest prayers, desires, thoughts or hopes.

So here's what I want to say to you: No matter how big you're hoping, whatever your desires are, God has something bigger that he can do in your life. He really can, so stay in there. Isn't it funny how we *over* estimate what we can do in one year's time? I mean, it seems to me that I have these big goals in January. Before I know it, twelve months fly by. It seems like a year will fly by and often times we over estimate what we can do in a twelve month period of time. Isn't it funny though, how we will *under* estimate what we can do and accomplish in a decade or two? I mean if you give a guy twenty, thirty, forty years to do something, oh he can change the world. Think about how much things have changed in the past ten or twenty years. We have iPads and Kindles. Did you realize in 2004 we really didn't have those? We had Palm Pilots and they don't even exist anymore. Today we have new technology, things are changing and I want to encourage you, God can do some great things in your life if you just don't quit; if you stay in there. If you give Him time in your life; don't expect everything to happen all in one year, but live like you can do it all in one year.

Faith is the secret to achievement. What I mean by that is this; in order for you to really achieve, it takes faith. It takes you having faith. That means you're going to reach through the invisible of what you don't have and what doesn't exist yet and the dream that you have and the vision that you have; you're going to reach through and you're going to take steps, do activities and take action to pull it in to the now.

Mark 9:23 Jesus said as far as possibilities go, everything is possible for the person who believes.

Be a student of belief, be a student of faith, be a student of possibility, of dreams and visions. Be a student of going forward and moving forward and watching your community change and reaching your nation and seeing prosperity come, even when outwardly it looks like it's the opposite that's happening. I want you to know it can turn around.

You know I told you about the bumper stickers and the fish and once in a while people will think they're a Christian because of certain things. I even have people say *"Well so and so's a Christian."* You can tell if someone is a Christian or you can tell if someone is in faith by the way they live their life, really. I mean I'm not the judge; I thank God that I'm not the judge, but let me ask you something. Do you ever see them read their Bible? Do you ever hear them pray? Do you ever see them go to church? Do you ever see them tithe? Oh, those are the habits of a person of faith. They do that... people of faith go to church, people of faith read their Bible, people of faith read and pray and have conversations. Let me ask you this; do they hang out with other Christians? People of faith hang out

with other Christians. So I'm not saying they are or they're not, I'm just asking you. You can tell if you look closely enough.
Jesus said that you can judge a tree by the fruit that it produces.
Why am I bringing this up? Because for you, the overcomer that you are and where you're going as an overcomer, I want to encourage you as the overcomer that you are. Don't tip-toe through life. Don't just try to arrive at your grave safely. This walk of faith, this fight of faith that we are in, this race that we are in, this

Christian race called the walk of faith, requires our passion. It requires our effort, our energy to study, to grow, to increase. Are you with me? Somebody can say that health is a priority for them or family is a priority for them. If I were to say health is a priority, well then you should be able to ask me, do you try to eat right? Do you try to exercise? Do you try to get plenty of sleep? If you were to say family is a priority I should be able to say to you, do you spend time with your spouse? Do you spend time with your children? Because if it is a priority than those things should be evident.

That's what I'm saying about our faith, we should be able to not just say we're in faith, we should be able to look at each other and go you're in faith, I can see that there's evidence that you're in faith, you're walking this walk, you're doing the do of the faith side of it. Are you with me? Faith makes us willing to take risk, faith risk and to even risk failure. Did you know failure is not falling down? Failure is not when the business closes. Failure is not that something went wrong. Failure is when you don't try at all. Failure is when you quit. Failure is when you sit on the couch and don't even get in the game… that's when you fail. You're in the game and you're trying, you're moving forward, you're taking faith risk and you're doing it.

I love the story of the three Hebrew hillbillies, Shadrach, Meshach and Abednego.

I love those guys. They were thrown in a fiery furnace and the scripture says in Daniel 4:17, "*They said this, if we're thrown into the blazing furnace, the God we serve is able to save us and he will rescue us.*" That's a faith statement all right. "*He will rescue us from your handle King, and even if he doesn't, we want you to know something King; we will not serve your God or worship the image you've set up."* I love that attitude. I love it because that is you doing your best and leaving the rest to God. And you know what? If I did and I tried, if I went for it and did not get through, I never lose because I'm going forward with you.

I tell you, when I lose is when I compromise and quit. I buckle under because the problem was too big, the obstacle was too big, the threat was too big and fear got the best of me. The enemy's way into our life is through fear and I want you to know something, you don't have anything to be afraid of in God, you're going to get through what you're going through. You are going to make it and you're not going to fail as long as you stay in the game.

An overcomer, his faith never gives up, he never quits.

Psalm 31:24 Be brave, be strong, don't give up, expect God he will be here soon!
Let me just stop and talk to you. I know this is true, that many of you are going through different things in your life.

Some of you are going through relationship stuff, some financial stuff, some business stuff, some stuff with your kids; we're all going through stuff. It's part of life. That's why we're overcomers we have to have adversity that we have to overcome. If we didn't have any adversity, if we didn't have anything to overcome, then we wouldn't be overcomers. The fact that we have some resistance is what makes us winners and champions. There is an adversary; there is an obstacle for us. Many of us despise our adversary, the doctor's report, the financial situation or the marriage problems. We despise it, but instead of wasting your energy despising that, spend your energy on overcoming and not quitting, not letting it defeat you.

In fact, declare this about yourself, I will not be defeated. I will not be defeated. If I fall down I'm getting back up. The scripture says be brave, be strong, don't give up, expect God, he'll be here soon. *Psalms 119:109 My life hangs in the balance, but I will not give up.*

Be a student of winners. Watch people who just don't quit.

Proverbs 24:16 Even if good people fall down seven times they will get back up.

This is a word for you if you're in that place right now, if you're there and you're saying *"Pastor, you don't know, you don't understand, you don't understand, I am tired, I am worn out."* I do understand that we get tired, I understand we get worn out, but God has a word for you in Galatians 6:9, *"Let us not get tired of doing what is right for after a while we will reap a harvest of blessing if we don't get discouraged and give up."* So come on, you can make it another day, all you have to do is get to tomorrow and his mercies are new every morning.

I don't know if you've ever had just a horrible day where you thought you couldn't make it through? And I mean the day almost crushed you; you ever been there before? I think we've all been there. But isn't it funny how you get through that day and you get into the next day or the next day after that and all of a sudden it eases a little bit, and you thought man it was horrible, I almost didn't make it there, but I didn't quit. I took a nap, went to bed, prayed with someone, stayed up all night, read my Bible, and sang all night, whatever. And here I am today, it's two days later, I'm still here, I made it. Five years later you look back and you go, I've really come a long way.

If you're in that place of hurt and heartache and you are broken and you're weak and you're tired and you're worn out, get through today. Just get with your brothers and sisters make some friends at church, serve, get in a support group, volunteer, go to a prayer ministers. Go connect, connect, connect, connect with someone because there's something about the strength from another person that says hey I've been through that, I know what that's like, I'm here with you. Even if they say, I haven't been through it, I can't imagine it, but I'm going to pray with you. Hang in there.

Faith reveals the overcomer that is on the inside of you. I tell you this all the time and I hope you don't get tired of hearing it, but I hope you receive it; there is an overcomer in you. How do I know that? Because you've got a Savior and he's living in you! There's an overcomer who lives on the inside of you if you're a Christ follower, you're a Christian, you've received him, he lives in you, you're more than a conqueror, not because you're a good person, but because Jesus lives in you and when you yield your heart to him and you become a student of the game of life. You build your faith, everybody's been given the measure of faith; every Christian has the measure of faith. Now here's what you do with the measure of faith. You take that faith, it's like having a muscle, and you begin to work your faith and work it and test it and examine yourself, take measurements, do the body caliper and see how much flabby fat you have. Spiritually, we're talking spiritual here, not physical.

Spiritually speaking, test yourself. Test your faith. Examine your faith. Study your faith. See if you're in the game. See if you're really living up to the measurement of a person who not only acknowledges Christ, but you acknowledge and live. The book of James is all about that.

1 John 5:4 Everyone who has been born of God has won the victory over the world; our faith is what wins the victory over the world.

So if you have Christ living in you, the Savior lives in you; you have God in you, how do you overcome the world? Because you have faith... develop your faith, work your faith become a student of the game. You're an overcomer. The overcomer, the overcomer lives in you. You're the little overcomer because the big overcomer lives in you. You're a student of the game, grow your faith, expand your faith, study faith, study the word, encourage one another, build each other up, lift one another up, you're winners, you're champions. Faith, true faith always takes action. Faith doesn't just talk about the dream. Have you ever met people that get ready to get ready to get ready to get ready? They take all the seminars, they go to all the courses, the read all the books and they get ready to get ready and someday I plan on, someday I'm going to. Here's the philosophy I want to teach you: Ready, Fire, Aim! What does that mean? Well, ready, fire, aim means this; do it as you do it. Don't get ready to get ready. You'll get ready as you do it. You will become as you do.

Whenever I was an electrician, the first day on the job, I mean I didn't go to school, they didn't send me to school to be an electrician; they sent me on the job. And I was scratching my head going this is crazy because I didn't know anything about it. I mean I knew a little bit from my own study, but they paired me up with another guy that did know everything. And you know what he did? He asked if I knew how to bend conduit. I laughed and shook my head no, telling him that it was my first day. And he said that he was going to teach me how to bend conduit and he showed me that you extend on half inch conduit you extend six inches out past the end of the mark if you're going to bend a ninety degree angle and then you put your weight on the bender and you pull it back. You put your level on it and he taught me the first day. I went home the first day, I knew how to bend conduit a little bit. I wasn't an expert, but a little bit.

A lot of people do it differently in their life. They want to go do classroom theory and study it and study it and study it and there's nothing wrong because I did go to school; one day a week and the other four days I worked. And what I want to say to you is yes you study, but the best way is to study, work and take action. Study, work, take action! See if you're really going to be an overcomer and this is where this whole series has been rah, rah, rah, you're an overcomer, dream big, change your self-talk, have a plan, have a goal, set goals, but see what this all boils down to is if you're really going to be the overcomer you don't have to understand everything. You don't have to have it all under your belt, you don't have to say well I'll tithe when I understand tithing; I'll tithe once I get my money in order, I'll tithe when... No, you don't understand it; you just begin to by faith live it out.

I've discovered that when you begin to live it out, you live it out and you walk it out, the understanding comes so much more quickly because let me tell you, those first few conduits that I bent, I didn't put enough weight into it and the pipe kinked and bit, but I learned to cut it off and start over. A righteous man will fall and make mistakes, but he'll get back up. You're a winner, you're a champion of faith, don't be afraid. Take those risks, love someone, start the class, start the ministry, pray, give, get involved, do His business, do His bidding, do it now, now faith is the substance.

James 2:20 When will you ever learn that believing is useless without doing what God wants you to do? Faith that does not result in good deeds is not real faith at all.

How do you know when faith is real? When there is a product produced from that faith. When there's activity. Love the environment of the kingdom of God, love his word, love praising and worshipping him, love people because people are what matters most. You want to get close to the heart of God? Begin to love people.

I love you and this is my prayer for you, Overcomer.

Father, we come before you, without you Father we are hopeless people. But because of you and because of what you've done for us and who you are and because of the blood of Jesus and because you live in us there's a Savior living in us. We are overcomers; I pray for each and every person who this message reaches. Father I pray for everyone in the name of Jesus, I ask that your Holy Spirit and your hand would touch their lives, encourage those that are hurting, strengthen those that are weak, bless those who need blessing and Father in the name of Jesus I pray that any discouragement would be lifted off; any hurt, any heartache, those that need healing, touch them and I pray and I ask you Father to help them stay another day to never quit, to never throw in the towel, to keep on pressing, to keep on keeping on, in Jesus' name we pray. Amen!

Now get out there and do some Overcoming!

More Books from this Author

The Secret to Blended Family Marriage and Parenting Success

Check it out on Amazon.

About the Author

With a passion for life and a desire to help people reach their full potential, Daren Carstens is pastor of Enjoy Church, a multi-denominational, multi-campus church serving the greater St. Louis area. As an author, speaker, and mentor, Daren is the son of an often-travelling pastor and has a background in construction, retail, and leadership development. Daren mixes his humorous, encouraging, and energetic style with practical real-world experience, which has allowed him to reach thousands of people every week through the church's physical locations, an online campus, and weekly television programs.

Daren and his wife Laura have a blended family consisting of 5 children and 4 grandchildren. They are excited to share their experiences in order to help and support others with blended families.

You can find more information on Daren by viewing one of his social media pages or by visiting his church website.

www.facebook.com/DarenWCarstens
www.twitter.com/DarenCarstens
www.daren.tv
www.Enjoychurch.tv

Questions or Comments for the Author

Daren would love to hear your thoughts. Email at
assistant@daren.tv

Would you like to receive my free newsletter?
Sign Up at www.daren.tv

View Other Books by Daren Carstens
Go to www.daren.tv

Request for speaking engagement
Contact: Request@daren.tv

Hear Daren Speak live online at
www.Enjoychurch.tv

One Last Thing

Would you take the opportunity to rate the book and share your thoughts through an automatic feed to your Facebook and Twitter accounts? If you believe your friends would get something valuable out of this book, I would be honored if you would share your thoughts. Also if you feel strong about the impact this book has made on your life. I would be thankful to you, if you would post a review on Amazon.

All the best,

Daren

www.ingramcontent.com/pod-product-compliance
Lightning Source LLC
Chambersburg PA
CBHW051830040426
42447CB00006B/460